P9-EME-978

THE PROPERTY OF

Palmerston Ave. Public School

WHITBY, ONT.

FLAGS
OF THE WORLD

This book aims not only at enabling the reader to recognize the world's flags, but at conveying some of their interest and revealing the light they throw on the story of mankind. Although many flags are severely practical, denoting a vessel's nationality or conveying a message, flags also form an essential part of heraldry, which has aptly been described as 'the shorthand of history'.

A few stirring episodes associated with flags are illustrated in the following pages, and if space had allowed many others would have been depicted. In all probability, there is not a country in the world whose story does not inspire its people to regard their flag with pride.

The descriptions of flags in this book represent the latest information available at the time of going to print.

A GROSSET ALL-COLOR GUIDE

FLAGS OF THE WORLD

BY I. O. EVANS
Illustrated by Jack and Enid Hayes

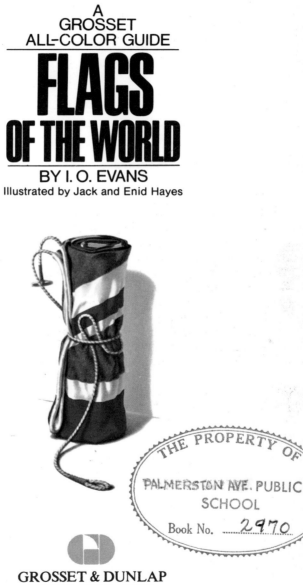

THE PROPERTY OF
PALMERSTON AVE. PUBLIC
SCHOOL
Book No. 2970

GROSSET & DUNLAP
A NATIONAL GENERAL COMPANY
Publishers · New York

THE GROSSET ALL-COLOR GUIDE SERIES
SUPERVISING EDITOR ... GEORG ZAPPLER
Board of Consultants

RICHARD G. VAN GELDER · Chairman and Curator, Mammals, American Museum of Natural History

WILLIAM C. STEERE · Director, New York Botanical Gardens

SUNE ENGELBREKTSON · Space Science Co-ordinator, Port Chester Public Schools

JOHN F. MIDDLETON · Chairman, Anthropology, New York University

CARL M. KORTEPETER · Associate Professor, History, New York University

MICHAEL COHN · Curator, Cultural History, Brooklyn Children's Museum

FRANK X. CRITCHLOW · Consulting Engineer, Applied and Theoretical Electronics

Copyright © 1970 by Grosset & Dunlap, Inc.
All Rights Reserved
Published Simultaneously in Canada
Copyright © 1970 by The Hamlyn Publishing Group Ltd.
Library of Congress Catalog Card No.: 78-120606
Printed in the United States of America

CONTENTS

INTRODUCTION

Early flags

Although the origin of flags is unknown, they have never served merely as decoration. Their age-old purpose is to symbolize communities and their leaders. The earliest emblems were not flags as we know them today, but poles tipped with images or other symbols. Such emblems were used in the ancient civilizations of Egypt, Babylon, Assyria, India and China.

Under the Romans their use became more systematic. The legions bore their familiar eagles and their *vexilla*, squares of cloth hanging from a crossbar on a staff and perhaps depicting the reigning emperor.

The coming of Christianity produced new symbols. In about A.D. 300 the Emperor Constantine was inspired by a vision to replace his own portrait on the military standard with the image of Christ or with the sacred monogram formed from the Greek letters *X* and *P, chi* and *rho,* which are the first part of the word 'Christos'. This standard was hereafter called a *labarum.*

The *signum,* earliest standard of the Roman army, was used by centurions for rallying troops.

4

Other flags, similarly inspired by visions, bore crosses, other religious symbols or representations of the saints, and these were taken into battle, too, especially during the Crusades. Some were flown from tall iron-sheathed masts mounted on four-wheeled frames, so that they could advance with the conquerors in victory or be rushed into a place of safety in defeat. That used in 1138 at the Battle of the Standard carried the emblems of three English saints.

Flags of various types, displaying their owners' armorial bearings, indicated the presence of persons of rank. These flags formed rallying points in battle, and because to capture such a trophy was regarded as a triumph and to lose it a disgrace, the fighting around them was especially fierce. Indeed the fall of an important flag might decide the outcome of an entire battle.

Heraldry
During the Middle Ages the designing of flags became a part of heraldry, which has its own specialized terms and a strict code of rules.

The *vexillum* was the standard of the Roman legionary cavalry and later of the veteran corps.

Heraldic tinctures

or   argent   azure   gules

sable   vert   purpure   tenné

ermine   erminois

The overlays are 'hatching', a shorthand system devised by seventeenth-century engravers to convey color in black and white.

In heraldry, yellow and white are not 'colors': they are 'metals' and are described as *or* (gold) and *argent* (silver). The heraldic colors in Britain are *gules* (red), *azure* (blue), *vert* (green), *sable* (black) and *purpure* (purple). Usage in the rest of Europe adds *tenne* (orange or tawny). There are also several 'furs', notably *ermine* (white with black mottlings) and *vair* (a pattern alternately white and blue).

Heraldic usage demands that two colors or two metals must never appear side by side on a flag; they must be separated by a narrow strip of metal between two colors, or color between two metals, known as a fimbriation or fringe.

Emblems from two flags may be combined by dimidiating or halving them, as in the Cinque Ports flag (page 72). To symbolize a royal marriage they may be impaled, placed side by side with the husband's nearer the flagstaff, as in the Queen Mother's personal standard (page 60). A more usual method of combining emblems is to quarter them; the system of quartering two, three, and four emblems is shown on pages 55 and 56.

(*Above*) arrows indicate the white fimbriation on the Union Jack. Designed according to heraldic principles, the two colors red and blue are separated by a 'metal', *argent*. (*Right and below*) two of the ways dictated by heraldic usage for combining emblems from different flags. Dimidiating results in the strange lion-cum-herring beast upon the flag of Yarmouth (*right*), and quartering in the state flag of Maryland (*below*).

7

Becket and toggle (*left*) and the Inglefield clip (*right*)

Modern flags

Traditionally made of bunting, a woolen cloth woven in Yorkshire in nine-inch widths, flags may now consist of a nylon-woolen mixture manufactured to many different measurements, but they are still measured by the older usage, a flag of 'eight breadths' being two yards wide.

The ropes to which the flags are sewn end just above the cloth, but a foot or so below it, so that even in a bad light flags are unlikely to be flown upside-down. A toggle or large wooden pin is secured to the rope above the flag, and this fastens through a rope loop or becket on the halyards, whereas the rope below the flag ends in a becket which fastens around a toggle on the halyards. In the British Royal Navy Inglefield clips enable flags to be fastened to, or detached from, the halyards very quickly, but to hold quite firmly.

The modern standard is what was formerly called a banner—a rectangular flag symbolizing a monarch or a president and displaying his or her arms. A flag ending in a swallowtail is normally called a burgee, and one that tapers gently to a point is a pendant or pennant; sometimes, however, these terms are reversed. One tapering more abruptly is simply called a triangular flag.

A country's national flag is that used by its government and sometimes by its citizens; its merchant flag is that worn by all vessels not in government service. A flag flown at a vessel's stern is her ensign, but as the British ensigns include the Union Flag in the canton—the upper part of the flag in the hoist, the half next to the flagstaff—the term 'ensign' is also applied to a flag of this type. A flag flown on the jackstaff at a vessel's bows is her jack.

Flag usage and etiquette

Because of their symbolism and their associations, flags are treated with respect by all considerate people, and in some countries their use is regulated by a formal flag code. Except

British merchant ships used to wear the Red Ensign at the stern and a house flag on the mainmast. Today, British merchant ships fly the pilot jack at the bows.

Flag at half-mast to signify mourning (*left*). Flag brailed, or rolled up and secured with halyards, for 'breaking out' (*right*).

when for special reasons they fly night and day, they are hoisted at sunrise and lowered at sunset, perhaps with a special ceremony.

A flag may be rolled up and secured with the halyards, so that it can be 'broken out' on reaching the masthead; or it may be hoisted unfurled, either briskly or with impressive slowness; it is always lowered slowly.

One national flag is never flown over another: a sign of conquest in war, this would most certainly be regarded as an insult in peace. Flags flown side by side should be at the same level, and as far as possible be of the same size. In front of or above a building, the place of honor is on the right facing the street.

Warships meeting at sea have their own special ceremonial; other vessels exchange salutes by 'dipping' their ensigns, lowering them and then rehoisting them in one movement.

To signify mourning, a flag is first raised to the top of the mast and then at once lowered to the half-mast position. Before being finally lowered at sunset it is again raised for a moment masthead high.

To strike a flag by lowering it completely is to surrender. To sail 'under false colors' is to fly the flag of a country to which the vessel does not belong.

A red flag is a sign of danger—or of revolution. A green flag normally means safety, but can give warning of a wreck. A yellow flag means quarantine. A white flag can denote surrender or ask for a truce. A black flag may indicate mourning; adorned with the white skull and crossbones it becomes the fearsome Jolly Roger, the pirate flag.

(*Left*) pirate flag (*top*); quarantine flag (*bottom*). (*Right*) a green flag denotes safety or, as here, warns of a wreck.

Raven flag of the Vikings.

LIBERTY TREE

AN APPEAL TO GOD

'Liberty Tree' flag.

NORTH AMERICA

The United States

Although the Raven flag of the Vikings may have been brought to 'Vineland the Good' by the Icelander Leif Ericson, the first European flags known to have been unfurled over American soil were those displayed by Columbus in 1492. Since he landed in the West Indies, these will be described later.

Other European flags flew for a time over the French colonies, Quebec and Louisiana; over the Swedish settlements on the Delaware; and over the New Netherlands on the Hudson. The British settlers in America also flew the emblems of their homeland. Among these was of course the contemporary Red Ensign, with the first Union Flag, combining the emblems of England and Scotland in the canton.

Some of the colonies had their own flags: the Beaver flag of New York symbolized the fur trade, while the Rattlesnake flag of South Carolina showed American defiance of British control. The rigid Puritans of New England, disliking the use of a cross upon a flag, devised their own emblems, some of which also suggest a distrust of British rule. The 'Liberty Tree' flag, a symbol of self-government, might bear the words 'An appeal to Heaven' or 'An appeal to God'.

At the Battle of Concord, which opened the War of Independence in 1775, the Americans are believed to have carried a flag that bore a great resemblance to the Parliamentary cavalry standard of the British Civil War; an arm emerging from a cloud and grasping a sword, with a Latin watchword signifying 'Conquer or die'.

Well known in American waters was the flag of the British East India Company; with the first Union Flag in the canton it bore from nine to thirteen red and white horizontal stripes in its fly. Whether the flag which the Americans first raised at Cambridge, Massachusetts, on January 1, 1776 was actually based on that of the East India Company is uncertain, but the resemblance is striking. It could have been devised independently, however, by placing six white stripes on the Red Ensign. In this Union Flag, also called the 'Congress flag', the thirteen stripes represented the thirteen states of the Union, while the British emblem in the canton showed some reluctance to break completely with the mother country.

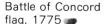

Battle of Concord
flag, 1775

Rattlesnake flag of South Carolina. Congress flag, Cambridge, 1776.

The Union flag of 1777 (*above, left*) had thirteen stars and stripes. Two more states joined the Union, hence the Union flag of 1795 (*above, right*). The Rattlesnake jack (*left*) is said to have been worn by 'vessels of war'.

After July 4, 1776, the people of the colonies felt the need for a national flag to symbolize their unity and independence. On June 14, 1777, Congress 'Resolved that the flag of the United States be thirteen stripes alternate red and white, that the Union be thirteen stars white in a blue field, representing a new constellation.'

As the exact arrangement of the stripes and stars was not specified, individual flagmakers used their own judgment, producing several variants. Meanwhile other flags appeared: 'vessels of war' are said to have worn a jack displaying a rattlesnake across thirteen red and white stripes, and merchantmen to have flown a flag only having thirteen stripes.

When Vermont and Kentucky were admitted into the Union in 1791 and 1792, respectively, the American flag had to be altered, and Congress enacted that 'from and after May 1, 1795 the flag of the United States be fifteen stripes and the Union be fifteen stars.'. It was this flag which inspired Francis Scott Key, when he saw it flying over Fort McHenry, to write what is now the American national anthem, 'The Star Spangled Banner'.

14

Francis Scott Key's moment of inspiration. Dawn comes, and the captive attorney, forced by the British to witness the attack on Fort McHenry, sees the American flag still flying over the fort.

15

The Stars and Bars, the first Confederate flag.

Confederate battle flag.

Flags of the Confederacy

When, in 1861, eleven of the states seceded from the Union they devised their own emblem. The first Confederate flag, adopted on March 5, 1861, was the Stars and Bars. While retaining the symbols dear to all Americans, it reduced the number of stars to seven, that of the states which first seceded, arranged them in a circle on a blue canton, and displayed on its fly three broad stripes, red, white and red.

This flag, however, was found to be impractical; its resemblance to the Stars and Stripes might lead to confusion in battle. A more distinctive emblem, although never legally adopted, soon won general approval: 'It was not the flag of the Confederacy, but simply the banner—the battle flag—of the Confederate soldier'. It displayed thirteen stars upon a blue cross, edged with white, on a red field.

Although satisfactory on land, the battle flag was ill-suited for naval use, as it could not be reversed to make a distress signal. It was therefore placed in the canton of an ensign with a plain white fly; in case this should be mistaken for a flag of truce, a broad red stripe was added in the fly.

Modern flags

Meanwhile new stars had been added in the canton of the American flag as new states were admitted into the Union, and so the Stars and Stripes evolved its present form. As the national and merchant flag and ensign of the United States, it now displays fifty stars in the canton — which forms the United States jack — while its fly retains the original thirteen stripes.

Whereas in Britain loyalty is centered on the Sovereign, in the United States it is focused upon the flag. To ensure uniformity in its use, a flag code was drawn up in 1923, and in 1942 it was legally established; it has also served as a basis for the similar codes of certain other countries. Two of its more important clauses run:

'The flag should never be used for advertising purposes in any manner whatsoever . . .' and 'The following is designated as the pledge of allegiance to the flag: "I pledge allegiance to the flag of the United States of America and to the Republic for which it stands, one Nation under God, indivisible, with liberty and justice for all"'.

The Stars and Stripes is the national and merchant flag, and ensign of the United States of America. It bears the thirteen stripes of the first Union flag but the stars in the canton now number fifty to represent the fifty states of the Union.

(*Right*) United States presidential flag.

(*Below*) United States yacht ensign.

The President of the United States is empowered to design his own flag, but its field is always blue. As presently in use, it displays the presidential seal: this shows the American Eagle grasping in its talons the emblems of peace and war, thirteen arrows and an olive branch, having thirteen leaves. Thirteen stars appear around its head, and it is surrounded by a circle of fifty stars, symbolizing the original and the present number of states in the Union. A shield of the national colors bearing seven white and six red stripes also appears, and the Latin motto *E Pluribus Unum* signifies 'From Many, One'. The flag of the Vice-President is somewhat similar, but its field is white. The heads of the various executive departments have their own appropriate flags.

The United States Navy flies the Stars and Stripes as its ensign and its fifty star canton as its jack. The warship pennant has seven white stars in its blue hoist; the fly is divided horizontally, red over white, and tapers gently to a split point. The 'official unofficial' homeward bound pennant is as long as the accessible material will allow. The church pennant, displaying a blue Latin cross on a white field, is the only flag

The District of Columbia has the same boundaries as Washington, the capital city of the United States which was named after the first President of the United States. Created to give Congress exclusive legislative powers over the seat of government, the District flies a flag (*above*) which derives appropriately from the arms of George Washington (*right*).

which may ever be flown above the Stars and Stripes, and then only during divine service.

Units of the United States Army have a national and a regimental standard or color. The standard of the United States Marine Corps displays on a red field the terrestrial globe showing the New World, surmounted by the American Eagle and placed in front of an anchor. The Stars and Stripes forms the colors of the United States Air Force.

United States yachts may be authorized to wear a special ensign whose blue canton displays thirteen stars arranged around a foul anchor. The ensign of the United States Power Squadron has a similar canton except that it is red; the fly contains thirteen blue and white vertical stripes.

The Coast Guard ensign and Customs Service flag display the eagle in the canton, blue on white, and sixteen vertical red and white stripes, with a suitable badge in the fly.

The flag of the District of Columbia, in which the American capital, Washington, is situated, derives from the arms of George Washington. It displays three red 'mullets'—the rowels of spurs—above two horizontal stripes, red on white.

19

Flags of the states

Each of the fifty states in the Union has its own flag, and although some of these emblems simply reproduce the state seal, others are of bold and original design.

The emblem of Alabama recalls in its pattern, though not in its color, the Confederate battle flag, in which it is thought to have its origin.

The flag of Alaska was chosen in open competition from a design submitted by a schoolboy; it represents the constellation of the Great Bear and the North Star.

Arizona's flag displays the colors of Imperial Spain, by which this region was once ruled, as well as those of the state itself; the coppery 'Arizona Star' is centered on a stylized view of the sun setting over the sea.

The stars on the flag of Arkansas recall the state's history. The three below its name indicate that at different times it has belonged to Spain, France and the United States; the upper star that it formed part of the Confederacy; and the stars surrounding the central white 'diamond', that it was the twenty-fifth state to be admitted to the Union.

Ruled by Spain and then by Mexico, California at last won its independence; the flag it then improvised, displaying a red star and a grizzly bear, was a basis for the design of its present emblem.

The sunshine, the blue skies and the snowy mountains of Colorado are represented on its flag by the golden disc within the letter 'C' and by the stripes of blue and white.

The three grapevines upon the shield on the flag of Connecticut recall the three English colonies which united to form this state; the Latin motto *Qui transtulit sustenit* could be translated 'He Who brought us over sustains us'.

The coat of arms on the flag of Delaware includes emblems of trade and agriculture; it shows the date, 'December 7, 1787', on which the state entered the Union.

The red cross on the flag of Florida also recalls the Confederate battle flag; the central device symbolizes the state's name and the arrival of Western civilization.

The flag of Georgia originally followed the Stars and Bars by having its fly striped horizontally, red, white and red, but the stripes have been replaced by the Confederate battle flag; the state seal appears in the hoist.

| Alabama | Alaska |

| Arizona | Arkansas |

| California | Colorado |

| Connecticut | Delaware |

| Florida | Georgia |

21

Hawaii

Idaho

Illinois

Indiana

Iowa

Hawaii, which became the fiftieth state of the Union in 1960, has been ruled by the United States since 1900, but it still keeps its original flag, which shows that it was formerly under British influence. The eight horizontal stripes represent the eight main islands in the Hawaiian Chain.

The supporters on the coat of arms shown on the flag of Idaho symbolize industry and freedom, the wheatsheaf represents agriculture and the Latin motto *Esto Perpetua* expresses the hope 'May she endure forever'.

Two national emblems, the American Eagle and a shield bearing the thirteen stars and stripes, appear on the seal and flag of Illinois; the motto reads 'State Sovereignty, National Union'.

After using the Stars and Stripes as its emblem, Indiana adopted its own state flag bearing the traditional symbol of knowledge, a flaming torch; the large star above this represents Indiana itself, the other stars, the eighteen states already in the Union when it was admitted.

Purchased by the United States from France, Iowa still flies the French tricolor with its central stripe broadened; here the American Eagle is shown with a scroll bearing the state motto: 'Our liberties we prize and our rights we will maintain'.

The seal shown on the flag of Kansas displays symbols recalling the state's development; above it is the state flower, and the Latin motto *Ad Astra per Aspera* signifies 'Through hardship to the stars'.

Kansas

The two men depicted on the seal and flag of Kentucky exemplify the motto 'United we stand, divided we fall'; the goldenrod shown is the state flower.

Kentucky

The flag of Louisana has been used since, and was probably inspired by, the War of 1812; the 'pelican in its piety', nourishing its young with its own blood, is a Christian symbol for self-sacrifice.

Louisiana

The state coat of arms on the flag of Maine includes the 'Liberty Tree'; the supporters represent agriculture and seamanship and the North Star symbolizes the Latin motto *Dirigo*, 'I direct'.

Maine

Dating from 1684, Maryland's flag bears the arms of Calvert, Lord Baltimore, who founded the state by royal charter.

The shields on the obverse and reverse of the flag of Massachusetts, respectively, depict an Indian warrior and the

Maryland

23

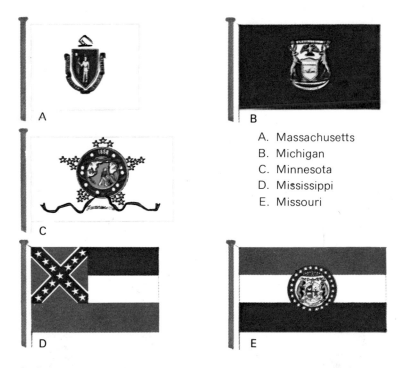

A. Massachusetts
B. Michigan
C. Minnesota
D. Mississippi
E. Missouri

'Liberty Tree'. The motto *Ense Petit Placidam sub Libertate Quietem* signifies 'With the sword she seeks peace in freedom'.

The landscape depicted on the flag of Michigan illustrates the motto *Si Quaeris Peninsulam Amoenam Circumspice,* 'If you seek a pleasant peninsula, look around you'. The word *Teubor*—'I will defend'—may recall the Anglo-American wars, for the state is on the Canadian frontier.

The flag of Minnesota is white on the obverse and blue on the reverse, and bears emblems of the retreat of the Indians and the spread of agriculture; the arrangement of the stars symbolizes the 'North Star State', *L'Etoile du Nord.*

The canton of the flag of Mississippi bears the Confederate battle flag; the three stripes in the fly recall the tricolor of France, from which the state was colonized.

The tricolor of France is also recalled by the flag of Missouri; the Latin motto on the seal *Salus Populi Suprema Lex Esto* means 'The people's welfare is the supreme law'.

The landscape depicted on the seal and flag of Montana

includes the symbols of agriculture and mining, the latter also being referred to in the Spanish motto *Oro y Plata,* 'Gold and Silver'.

That of Nebraska represents agriculture, craftsmanship and commerce by land and sea; the date shown, 'March 1, 1867', is that of the state's admission to the Union, and the motto reads 'Equality before the law'.

The words 'Battle Born' above the white star on the flag of Nevada recall that the Civil War was being waged when the state was admitted to the Union in 1864; the sagebrush below the star is the state flower.

The vessel depicted on the seal and flag of New Hampshire is the *Raleigh,* one of the first ships of the American Navy; the date is that of the Declaration of Independence.

The buff color of New Jersey's flag is said to be that chosen by George Washington for the emblems of his forces; the ploughs on the coat of arms represent agriculture, and the supporters exemplify the motto 'Liberty and Prosperity'.

A

A. Montana
B. Nebraska
C. Nevada
D. New Hampshire
E. New Jersey

D

B

C

E

25

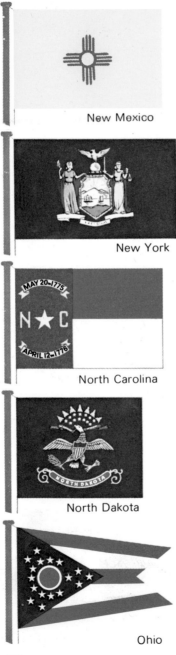

New Mexico

New York

North Carolina

North Dakota

Ohio

The emblem on the flag of New Mexico is the Zia sun-symbol of the state's aborigines, the Zuni Indians; the colors show that it was formerly ruled by Imperial Spain.

In the coat of arms which appears on the seal and flag of the state of New York the shield depicts a scene on the Hudson River; the supporters represent freedom and justice and the soaring eagle upon the globe which forms the crest symbolizes the motto *Excelsior,* 'Ever upward, higher'.

The flag of North Carolina suggests the first Confederate flag, the Stars and Bars; the dates of two important declarations of independence are shown in the hoist.

Two national emblems, the thirteen stars and the American Eagle, appear on the flag of North Dakota, which is believed to be derived from the colors of the state militia during the Spanish-American War of 1898.

In its design and colors the tapering burgee which forms the flag of Ohio recalls the Stars and Stripes; the stars indicate that this was the seventeenth state to be admitted to the Union and the circle suggests its colloquial name, the 'Buckeye State'.

The flag of Oklahoma displays two emblems of peace, the olive branch and the American Indian *calumet,* or peace pipe, crossed upon an Indian brave's shield, adorned with seven eagle's feathers.

The shield on the obverse of the flag of Oregon displays symbols of the departure of the British as the Americans arrive by land and sea; the reverse depicts a golden beaver.

Upon the flag of Pennsylvania appear the state's arms; the shield displays emblems of commerce and agriculture, also represented by the supporters—two farmhorses; the scroll bears the motto 'Virtue, Liberty, and Independence'.

As is shown by the thirteen gold stars on its flag, Rhode Island was among the states which formed the Union; the anchor is the time-honored symbol of hope.

One of the earliest revolutionary flags was that devised in 1776 by Colonel Moultrie, a crescent moon in the upper hoist of a dark blue field. With the addition of a palmetto tree, South Carolina adopted the Moultrie flag when it seceded from the Union in 1860.

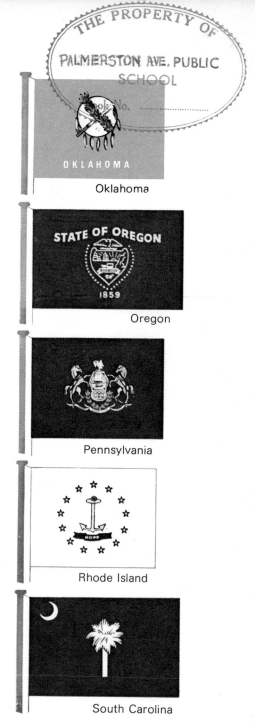

THE PROPERTY OF PALMERSTON AVE. PUBLIC SCHOOL Book No.

Oklahoma

Oregon

Pennsylvania

Rhode Island

South Carolina

27

The state seal which appears on the flag of South Dakota bears symbols of agriculture, industry and commerce; the sun emblem which surrounds it endorses the claim that this is the 'Sunshine State'.

The three white stars on the flag of Tennessee indicate that his was the third state, after the original thirteen, to be admitted to the Union.

After passing from the control of France to that of Spain, Texas was then ruled by Mexico; largely colonized by the Americans and English, it finally gained independence. It then adopted the flag which it retained after it was admitted to the Union—a fitting emblem for the 'Lone Star State'.

On the seal and flag of Utah, the American Eagle is shown grasping a symbol of industry, the beehive; the supporters are two American flags, and the dates are important in the history of the state of Utah. In 1847 the first Mormons entered and settled in Salt Lake Valley, and in 1896 the state was admitted to the Union.

The landscape depicted on the flag of Vermont includes the 'Liberty Tree' dominating the symbols of agriculture, and the motto is 'Unity and Freedom'.

The seal and flag of Virginia represent the armed figure of Virtue trampling underfoot the emblem of oppression; the Latin motto *Sic Semper Tyrannis* is appropriate: 'Thus ever to tyrants'.

As the state of Washington was named after the hero of America's independence, it seems fitting that his image should be depicted on its seal and flag.

The seal on the flag of West Virginia includes the emblems of freedom and the fight for freedom in addition to figures representing agriculture and mining; the motto *Montani Semper Liberi* makes the proud declaration 'Mountaineers forever free'.

The coat of arms on the flag of Wisconsin includes a shield depicting the implements of agriculture and industry; the supporters are a seaman and a farmer, the crest is a beaver, the historic thirteen stars appear on a scroll and the motto is 'Forward'.

The state seal of Wyoming appears on the figure of a buffalo silhouetted in white upon a flag of the traditional American colors, red, white and blue.

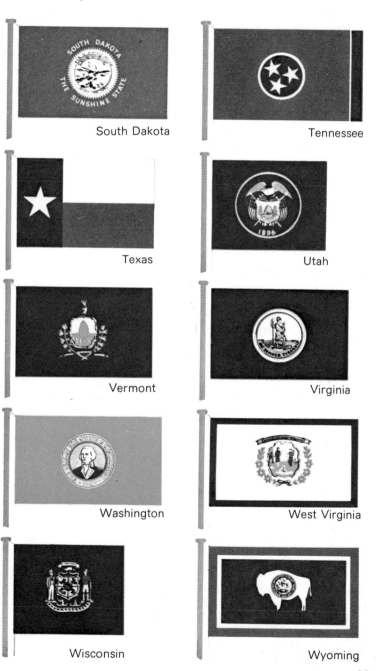

South Dakota

Tennessee

Texas

Utah

Vermont

Virginia

Washington

West Virginia

Wisconsin

Wyoming

29

(*Above*) national and merchant flag, ensign, and jack of Canada.

(*Right*) national arms of Canada.

Canada

Canada was the first overseas region of what was then the British Empire to be granted its own flag, in 1869. It was the Red Ensign displaying a shield in the fly which quartered the arms of Canada's first four provinces: Ontario, Quebec, Nova Scotia and New Brunswick. In 1921 the shield was replaced by another, of simpler but more effective pattern, bearing the arms of Canada itself; these combine the Lion of England, the Lion Rampant of Scotland, the Harp of Ireland and the Lilies of France with the Canadian Maple Leaf.

In 1965 this ensign was superseded by a new national flag, which is also the merchant flag, ensign and jack. The Canadian emblem, the red maple leaf, is displayed at its center on a white field, and there are broad red stripes down the hoist and fly.

A Queen's personal flag for Canada had already been approved in 1961; it centers the royal emblem on a flag displaying the arms of Canada, which are similar to those formerly shown on the Red Ensign. Its upper part resembles the royal standard, except that the English Lions in the fourth quarter are replaced by the French *fleurs-de-lis,* and below are three red maple leaves on a white field.

30

Approved in 1967, the flag of the Canadian armed forces places the national flag in the canton of a white flag, with the emblem of the armed forces in the fly. This includes the royal crown, the crossed swords of the army, the anchor of the navy and the flying eagle of the air force.

Since 1955 the Anglican Churches in Canada have had their own flag, a St. George's Cross, red on white, with a green maple leaf in each quarter; the arms of the appropriate diocese may be superimposed at the center of the cross.

Each of the provinces of Canada has its own flag; that of Quebec is older than the first of the Canadian flags.

The French-speaking inhabitants of Quebec have long honored their *Fleurdelise* flag, but this became the province's emblem only in 1948. It displays a broad white cross on a sky-blue field and has a white *fleur-de-lis* in each quarter. The arms of Quebec consist of a shield divided horizontally into three portions. In its upper part appear two *fleurs-de-lis*, blue on gold—later these were altered to three, gold on blue; at the center a lion, gold on red; and at the base three maple

Queen Elizabeth's personal flag for use in Canada.

Provincial flag of Nova Scotia.

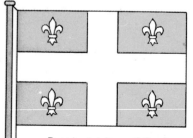

Provincial flag of Quebec.

31

Provincial flag of New Brunswick.

Provincial flag of Prince Edward Island.

leaves, green on gold. The shield is ensigned with the imperial crown, and a scroll bears the motto *Je Me Souviens,* which signifies 'I recall'.

The flag of Nova Scotia is based upon the arms which were granted to the province in 1626: a shield displaying the royal emblem of Scotland, the lion rampant and tressure, red on gold, at the center of a St. Andrew's Cross with its colors reversed, a blue cross on white. This well symbolizes the name of the province, which means 'New Scotland'.

Two provincial flags, both based on the badges formerly flown on the British ensign, display on the upper part of their fields the Lion of England, gold on red, as on the British royal standard. Below, that of New Brunswick bears a lymphad, an heraldic ship, black on gold, upon the blue and white wavy stripes which indicate the sea. On the lower part of the flag of Prince Edward Island is represented an island, upon which three saplings grow beside a large oak tree.

Newfoundland is Britain's oldest colony. Sir Humphrey

Gilbert took possession of the island in 1583. It long enjoyed dominion status but became the tenth province of Canada in 1949. Instead of creating a special flag, it still retains its former badge, which was approved in 1904; this appears at the center of the British Union Flag as the emblem of the lieutenant-governor. It depicts Mercury, the god of commerce, showing Britannia a fisherman who is offering the produce of the sea; the Latin motto signifies 'I bring you these gifts'.

This badge, placed on the British Union flag, represents the province of Newfoundland.

Two of the provinces fly the British Red Ensign, as did the Dominion of Canada itself at one time, but with the appropriate provincial, instead of the Canadian, shield in the fly.

The shield of the province of Ontario places the Cross of St. George, red on white, at its top, with three maple leaves on one stalk below, gold on a green field. This device was originally granted in 1868, but its use upon the Red Ensign was officially approved only in 1965. The shield of Manitoba also displays the St. George's Cross, red on white, but above a green field displaying a buffalo on a rock, all in natural colors. These arms were granted in 1905.

The province of Ontario places its badge (*above*) on the British Red Ensign.

Another provincial badge worn on the British Red Ensign is that of Manitoba.

The provincial arms appear on Saskatchewan's centennial banner.

On the blue field of Alberta's provincial flag is this shield.

Provincial flag of British Columbia.

The centennial banner of Saskatchewan, although it has not yet received official approval, was first flown in 1965 to celebrate the Jubilee of the province. Its colors, red, green and gold, symbolize the fires that used to sweep the prairies, the luxuriant vegetation and the fields of ripening wheat. The latter is also represented by the sheaf of wheat in the hoist and by the three stylized wheatsheaves upon the shield in the fly, below the lion, red on a gold field, which recalls the ties of the province with Britain; these arms date from 1906.

Alberta also has a provincial banner, but its design is simpler: upon a royal blue field are placed the arms of the province, which were granted in 1907. They consist of a shield on which appears a St. George's Cross, red on white, to represent the ties with Britain, and below, against the blue sky, a range of snow-covered mountains which symbolize the distant Rockies. In front of the mountains are a line of hills, a prairie and a cornfield.

The flag of British Columbia, the most westerly province of Canada, places the Union Flag, with a gold crown at its center, above the heraldic symbols for the sun and sea, to represent the sun setting over the Pacific. It is based on the arms granted in 1906.

Canada has two territories. The provincial flag of the Yukon Territory was approved in 1967, but the arms which it displays were granted in 1956. They appear on the central stripe of a vertical tricolor, forest green, snow white and lake blue, and consist of a shield whose upper part depicts a St. George's Cross, with a circle of *vair* at its center to symbolize the British fur traders, while the lower part bears symbols of two snow-covered, gold-bearing mountains separated by the Yukon River. The crest is a malamute dog upon a mound of snow, and on the flag the shield appears above a wreath of fireweed.

In 1969 the Northwest Territories adopted a new flag, placing the territories' badge on a white field with a blue bar in the hoist and fly. This is a shield crossed near the top by wavy lines, blue on white, symbolizing the Northwest Passage through the eternal snows; a diagonal wavy line below represents the 'timber line' between the forests and the tundra, whose respective emblems are gold rectangles on a green field and the mask of an arctic fox.

Yukon's arms (*below, left*) appear on a tricolor, those of the Northwest Territories (*below, right*) on another.

Pan-American Union flag.

CENTRAL AND SOUTH AMERICA

The Caribbean

Where Columbus made his first landing in the Americas is uncertain—it may have been on Watling Island in the Bahamas. Later he discovered the two largest islands in the Caribbean, Cuba, which he at first mistook for Japan, and Haiti, which, in honor of the Spanish monarchs who had made his venture possible, he called Hispaniola.

Wherever it was accomplished, his landing was made with great pomp and circumstance; clad in scarlet, he himself bore the royal standard of Spain, quartering the golden castle on red of Castille with the red lion on silver of Leon. His ships' captains, also richly attired, carried a white banner bearing a green cross and the letters 'F' and 'Y', for Fernando and Ysabel.

It seemed appropriate that when, in 1932, the Pan-American Union decided to express in a flag its ideal of achieving solidarity throughout the whole of the New World, this should pay tribute to Columbus's achievement. His flagship, the *Santa Maria,* is represented by a central cross, behind which gleams the traditional 'Bronze sun of the Incas', and his two other vessels, the *Pinta* and the *Nina,* by the two smaller crosses flanking it.

When the Cubans' long struggle for independence from Spain began about 1850, their exiled leader asked a comrade to design a suitable flag. This emblem, *La Estrella Solitaria,*

The first European flags in America. Columbia and his ships' captains go ashore bearing the royal standard of Spain and a flag charged with the initials of their patrons, Fernando and Ysabel.

Cuba: national and merchant flag
and ensign.

Haiti: national flag and ensign.

Dominica: national flag
and ensign.

'The Solitary Star', has become the national and merchant flag and ensign of Cuba now that independence has been achieved. Designed in 1849 by two exiles living in New York City, its three blue stripes represent the three provinces into which the country was divided in colonial times. The three sides of the triangle stand for liberty, equality and fraternity.

The western part of the island which Columbus called Hispaniola is now known as Haiti. When its Negroes rose in revolt against their white rulers, their leader is said to have ripped the white stripe from the French tricolor, leaving the blue to represent the Negroes and the red, the mulattos. The merchant flag of Haiti is now halved vertically, black and red; the national flag and ensign shows at its center the weapons of war grouped around a palm tree.

The eastern part of the island now forms the Dominican Republic. Its merchant flag is quartered blue and red by a white cross, and the national flag and ensign places the country's arms at the center of the cross.

Recently some of the West Indian islands within the British Commonwealth have achieved independence, and a number have exchanged badges on the Blue Ensign for their own flags.

On becoming independent within the Commonwealth in 1962, Jamaica adopted a national flag bearing a gold cross; it is black in the hoist and fly and green at the top and bottom. On the Queen's personal flag for Jamaica, approved in 1966, the royal emblem is centered on a St. George's Cross shown with a golden pineapple on each of its arms.

When Jamaica became independent, its former dependency, the Cayman Islands, became a British colony and now places its own badge on the Blue Ensign. This includes local emblems, such as a turtle and a pineapple plant, as well as the Lion of England and the text 'He hath founded it upon the seas'.

The badge of the Leeward Islands, which includes a large pineapple, was designed by the group's former Governor, Sir Benjamin Pine. Female figures appear on the badges of the British Virgin Islands and Montserrat. Antigua and St. Kitts-Nevis, also within the Leewards, have recently chosen new flags of striking design.

Also achieving their independence in 1962, Trinidad and

Jamaica: national flag.

Antigua: national flag.

St. Kitts-Nevis: national flag.

Trinidad and Tobago: national flag.

Barbados: national flag.   Dominica: badge on the British Blue Ensign.

Tobago selected a new national flag with a black stripe, fimbriated with white, crossing a red field from the top of the hoist to the bottom of the fly. On the Queen's personal flag for these islands, approved in 1966, the royal emblem almost obscures a representation of one of Columbus's three ships, white on blue, which appears below two hummingbirds, white on black.

Barbados, near the Windward Islands, formerly displayed on its badge a picture of Britannia ruling the waves. Since the island obtained independence within the Commonwealth in 1966, the broken-off head of the trident reflects the country's seafaring tradition and symbolizes the island's break with Britain.

The badge of the Windward Islands places a shield, quartered red, yellow, green and white, within a garter surmounted by the royal crown; the Latin motto *I Pede Fausto* signifies 'Go with a fortunate foot'.

40

The new badge of Dominica, approved for use on the Blue Ensign in 1965, consists of the island's coat of arms. The shield bears the emblems of a coconut palm, a Dominican *crapaud* or edible toad, a carib canoe and a banana tree; the supporters are two parrots and the crest is the Lion of England. The motto in the local patois *Après Bondie c'est la Terre* means 'After the Good Lord we love the soil'.

Two other islands within the Windward group adopted flags in 1967. That of Grenada is a horizontal tricolor, blue, yellow and green; a sprig consisting of two leaves and a nutmeg is displayed at the center. That of St. Lucia replaces its former badge—a black shield bearing a device in which two lengths of cane quartered two roses with two *fleurs-de-lis,* representing the claim that the French once made to this island; it is a blue flag bearing a black triangle bordered with white and with a yellow triangle at its base.

The badge of St. Vincent, showing two female figures at an altar, with the Latin motto *Pax et Justitia,* 'Peace and Justice',

Grenada: national flag.

St. Lucia: national flag.

St. Vincent: badge on the British Blue Ensign.

41

Puerto Rico: national flag.

is still in use, but it is proposed to supersede this by a flag resembling that of Grenada with stripes of tartan green, yellow and blue, and a central device representing a sprig of leaves and berries.

Puerto Rico changed hands after the Spanish-American War of 1898, and in 1952 it became a self-governing commonwealth within the United States of America. Its national flag is that borne by the island's patriots when with the Cubans they revolted against Spanish rule; it is identical with the flag of Cuba except that its colors are reversed. The flag of the governor-general is white, and represents in the hoist the seal granted in 1511 by Ferdinand and Isabella of Spain; its ornate design includes a number of religious symbols.

The flag of the American Virgin Islands is white and bears two United States emblems: the American Eagle and a red, white and blue shield carrying thirteen stripes. In the hoist and fly respectively there appear the letters 'V' and 'I'.

Though some distance from Jamaica, the Turks and Caicos Islands, like the Cayman Islands, were one of its dependencies and, again like the Caymans, they became a separate British colony when Jamaica gained independence in 1962. Their former badge, which appeared on the Blue Ensign, depicted a native at work on a beach near some huts, with a three-masted sailing ship in the offing. Their present badge, which also appears on the Blue Ensign, consists of a gold shield displaying three of the products of this group of islands: a Queen conch shell, a spiny lobster and a Turk's head cactus.

Separating the Caribbean Sea from the Atlantic is a group

of islands called the Bahamas. Its badge, which appears on the Blue and the Red Ensign, represents a British vessel chasing two pirate ships which are about to disappear over the horizon. This scene is surrounded by a garter emblem bearing the Latin motto *Commercia expulsis piratis restituta,* which can be translated 'Commerce restored by the defeat of the pirates'; the garter is surmounted by a crown, and at the foot of the badge is a scroll bearing the word 'Bahamas'.

Even farther out in the Atlantic, to the northeast of the Caribbean, is the group of islands known as the Bermudas, Shakespeare's 'still-vexed Bermoothes'. Their badge appears on the Red Ensign and consists of a shield on which a lion is shown grasping another more ornate shield which bears a representation of an event important in the island's colonization: the wreck—in 1609 when the group was still uninhabited—of Admiral Sir George Somers's vessel, the *Sea Venture,* on a reef which is still known as Sea Venture Flat.

Turks and Caicos Islands: former badge on the British Blue Ensign.

Bahamas: badge on the British Blue and Red Ensigns.

Bermuda: badge on the British Red Ensign.

México and Central America

The southern part of the New World was long ruled by Spain, and when the Spanish Empire fell it was divided into a number of independent republics.

Until recently, the merchant flag of Mexico did not bear the national arms, but it has now been brought into line with the national flag and ensign. Hence the Mexican flag is a vertical tricolor of green, white and red, bearing its arms at the center; these are based on the Aztec legend that an eagle standing on a cactus and holding a serpent in its beak would reveal the

The national arms of the Mexican flag recall the event shown above.

44

place where the tribe might settle.

The isthmus south of Mexico was for a time united as the Central American Federation, and its five nations still use variants of the Federation's flag, which was striped horizontally, blue, white and blue.

Guatemala keeps the same colors, but has rearranged them to run vertically. Its merchant flag, therefore, bears three vertical stripes, blue, white and blue; as is usual in Latin America, the national flag and ensign places the country's arms on the central stripe.

A city and an empire are born as the Aztec prophecy is fulfilled. Tenochtitlan was built on this swampy island, and with it the foundations of modern Mexico were laid.

The national flag and ensign of Guatemala. The bird is the quetzal, the national symbol for independence.

45

Honduras: national and merchant flag.

British Honduras: badge
on the British Blue Ensign.

El-Salvador: national flag
and ensign.

Honduras still uses the Federation flag, with the addition of a distinguishing emblem. The national and merchant flag bears five blue stars on the white stripe to express the hope that the five republics of Central America will again unite. The ensign replaces them with the national arms.

The badge of British Honduras, which appears in the fly of the Blue Ensign, is a shield divided into three sections, displaying the Union Flag, a woodman's implements, and a sailing vessel, the last two to represent the mahogany trade.

Like Honduras, El Salvador uses the flag of the old Federation suitably distinguished. The merchant flag places the words *Dios Union Libertad,* 'God, Unity, Freedom', on the central stripe, whereas the national flag and ensign incorporates these words into the arms displayed on that stripe.

The national and merchant flag and ensign of Nicaragua also places the national arms at the center of a flag striped horizontally, blue, white and blue, but the flag itself is longer than those of Honduras and El Salvador.

Costa Rica distinguishes its flags by placing a red stripe at the center of the flag of the Central American Federation. Its national and merchant flag is striped horizontally, blue, white, red, white, blue; the ensign as usual adds the national arms on the central stripe, but it places them toward the hoist.

The Republic of Panama was never within the Central American Federation. Formerly part of Columbia, it became independent only in 1903, and naturally its flag is totally different from any of those which once formed the Federation. Its national and merchant flag and ensign, which is quartered, has red, white and blue as its colors.

The Panama Canal Zone, through which that waterway runs, is in fact under United States jurisdiction. The shield displayed at the center of its dark blue flag is red, white and blue, and it includes the traditional thirteen stripes; below these a sailing vessel is shown passing through a narrow stretch of the canal. The motto runs 'The Land Divided, the World United'.

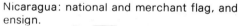

Nicaragua: national and merchant flag, and ensign.

Costa Rica: national and merchant flag, and ensign.

Panama: national and merchant flag, and ensign.

Ecuador: merchant flag.

Colombia: national flag.

Venezuela: national flag
and ensign.

South America

The hero of South American independence, Simon Bolivar, aimed not only at freeing the continent from Spanish rule but also at uniting it into one great republic. He succeeded only in liberating and uniting a stretch of territory in its northwest, but his Great Colombia Republic soon broke up into three separate nations. These still use the flag one of his followers designed to symbolize 'golden America as separated by the blue sea from the bloodthirsty rule of Spain'.

The merchant flag of Ecuador is a horizontal tricolor, yellow, light blue and red, with the upper stripe double the width of the other two. The national flag and ensign displays the country's arms in the center; these include a coastal scene, dominated by Mount Chimborazo, and an off-shore steamer, representing commerce.

The national flag of Colombia is similar to that of Ecuador, except that its central stripe is dark blue. The merchant flag places at its center a white star surrounded by a red-bordered blue oval; the ensign replaces this by the Colombian arms, which symbolize the Panama isthmus—formerly Colombian territory—separating the Atlantic and Pacific.

The Venezuelan merchant flag has the same colors as the flags of Ecuador, but its horizontal stripes are equal, and at its center is an arc of seven white stars. The national flag and ensign places the country's arms in the upper hoist: a shield representing agricultural wealth by a wheatsheaf, and the *llanos* (broad plains) by an untamed white horse.

The region to the east of Venezuela was formerly known as British Guiana, and it placed on the Blue Ensign a badge showing a three-masted ship with sails set, and a scroll bearing the Latin Motto *Damus Petimusque Vicissim,* which could be translated 'We both give and seek'. On becoming independent within the Commonwealth as Guyana, it adopted a flag showing two fimbriated triangles, one yellow and one brown, extending from the hoist of a green flag.

Surinam, Dutch Guinea, flies a white flag on which an oval black ring joins five stars of different colors. The Netherlands Antilles, off the Venezuelan coast, also fly a white flag, on which a blue horizontal stripe bearing six white stars is placed across a red vertical stripe.

(*Left*) Surinam: national flag.

(*Below*) Guyana: national flag.

Peru: national flag

Bolivia: national flag and ensign.

The flag of Peru, so different from the emblems of the countries farther north, which had belonged to the Great Colombia Republic, is reputed to have had a romantic origin. When freedom fighters, intent on liberating their country from the Spaniards, landed on its coast, a flock of birds is said to have soared aloft in fright—whereupon their leader, seeing the red and white plumage gleaming in the sun, shouted 'Behold the flag of liberty!' This inspired the merchant flag of Peru, which is striped vertically, red, white and red. There are two versions of the Peruvian arms; both include a llama, a tree and a cornucopia to symbolize the country's natural resources. Placed at the center of the merchant flag, the simpler form of the national arms converts it into the national flag, the more complicated into the ensign.

Bolivia, which at one time was known as Upper Peru, is named after Simon Bolivar. The three horizontal stripes upon its merchant flag, red, gold and green, are said to represent the country's animal, mineral and vegetable wealth. The national flag and ensign displays its arms on the central stripe;

these also symbolize that wealth by a llama, a tree, a wheat-sheaf and a house.

The national and merchant flag and ensign of Chile was designed by an American officer serving with the engineers of the Chilean Army. He was obviously intent upon producing a simplified version of the American flag, reducing its stars and stripes to the bare minimum, and he similarly followed United States practice in using the flag's canton as a jack. One white star also appears on Chile's arms; these are placed on the national flag to form the President's standard.

The red, white and blue horizontal tricolor of Paraguay, which was adopted by that country when it won its independence from Spain, is distinguished from that of the Netherlands by the badges placed at the center of the national and merchant flag and ensign. A different emblem appears on each of the flag's two sides: that on the obverse includes a gold star between wreaths of palm and olive, that on the reverse, a lion guarding the 'Cape of Liberty', the traditional emblem of a freed slave.

Chile: national and merchant flag, and ensign.

Paraguay: obverse of national and merchant flag, and ensign.

51

Argentina: national flag and ensign.

Uruguay: national and merchant flag, and ensign.

Although very similar to the flag of the Central American Federation, the emblem of the Argentine Republic is said to have derived its colors from those of the cockade worn by the nationalists during their fight for freedom. The merchant flag of Argentina is striped horizontally, light blue, white and light blue; the national flag and ensign displays at the center the 'Sun of May', whose sudden appearance through the clouds was regarded as a good omen for the newly independent state.

After gaining its freedom from Spanish domination, Uruguay was formed in 1828, through the mediation of Britain as a 'buffer state' between Brazil and the Argentine Republic. It shows its relationship with Argentina by the 'Sun of May' in the canton and the light blue and white stripes of its national and merchant flag and ensign.

The Falkland Islands, being within the British Commonwealth, place a badge depicting a blue shield within a white circle on the Blue Ensign. On its upper part appears a hornless ram, and below this are the wavy blue and white stripes which form the heraldic symbol for the sea; upon these is shown the vessel *Desire* in which John Davis was sailing when he discovered the Falklands. The motto, 'Desire the Right', is an obvious pun upon the ship's name.

While Columbus was discovering the New World on behalf of Spain, Portuguese explorers were rounding the Cape of Good Hope to investigate the lands farther east. Anxious to avoid disputes between the two leading Catholic powers, Pope Alexander VI decreed in 1493 that the meridian 100 leagues west of the Cape Verde Islands should become a frontier; all newly discovered lands to its east were to go to Portugal, all to its west to Spain. His intention was to assign the regions beyond the Cape to Portugal and all America to Spain, but the demarcation line was altered to 370 leagues in the Spanish-Portuguese treaty of the following year, so that the eastern part of South America was allocated to Portugal.

This included what is now Brazil, which retained the Portuguese language when it gained its independence. Its national and merchant flag and ensign is green, with a gold diamond at its center; upon this is displayed a celestial globe bearing a number of stars. An equatorial girdle bears the words *Ordem e Progresso,* 'Order and Progress'.

Falkland Islands: badge on the British Blue Ensign.

Brazil: national and merchant flag, and ensign.

53

GREAT BRITAIN AND NORTHERN IRELAND

British royal standards

For many centuries the English monarchs have flown their royal standards: the Dragon flag of King Harold and the gonfalon of William I are represented on the Bayeux Tapestry, which commemorates the Norman Conquest.

During the Crusades, Richard I of England won fame as Richard the Lionhearted, and he represented this title by depicting on his arms first one lion, and later three lions, gold on red; this formed the English royal standard until 1340.

In that year Edward III of England also claimed to be the rightful king of France, and he showed that he regarded this as the more important part of his joint realm by quartering the French royal arms, gold lilies strewn on a blue field, with the lions of England, giving the former precedence by placing it in the first and fourth quarters of his standard.

This flag remained in use for nearly a century, except that from 1377 to 1399 Richard II impaled this standard with the arms assigned to an earlier English king, Edward the Confessor — three martlets, heraldic birds like martins or swallows without feet, surrounding a cross.

When in 1365 Charles V of France reduced the number of lilies on his standard to three, Henry IV of England made a similar alteration on his own royal standard to show that he claimed not 'France Ancient' but 'France Modern'.

Upon her marriage to Philip of Spain in 1554, Mary I impaled her own arms with his; these quartered the Castle, gold on red, of Castile, with the Lion rampant, red on white, of Leon (page 36). After Mary's death in 1558 her successor, Elizabeth I, reverted to the Henry IV standard.

Elizabeth's successor, James I of England, was already James VI of Scotland, and in 1603, to represent all his kingdoms upon his standard, he quartered the arms of France and England, not only with the emblem of Scotland but also with that of Ireland. The former displayed a lion rampant surrounded by a double tressure or framework enriched at each side and corner with lilies, perhaps to recall Scotland's traditional friendship with France, all red on gold; the latter, devised by Henry VIII, represented a gold harp with silver strings on a blue field.

(*Opposite*) the Bayeux Tapestry displays two royal standards: Harold's Dragon flag (*left*) and William's gonfalon (*right*).

The course of English territorial ambitions in France can be traced in the standards of Edward III (*above, left*), Henry IV (*above, right*) and James I (*right*).

55

After the execution of Charles I in 1649, the royal standard went out of use, and when Oliver Cromwell became Lord Protector in 1653 he flew his own personal standard. This placed his arms, a silver lion on a black shield, at the center of a flag quartering the red cross on white of England with the white cross on blue of Scotland and the Irish Harp.

At the Restoration in 1660 no royal standard was available, so Charles II improvized a flag displaying a crown above his initials 'CR', in gold on white, at the center of the first Union Flag, which is described on page 62.

After James II abdicated in 1689, William III and his wife Mary, who ruled jointly, impaled their arms, but it is not certain whether this device was ever used as a flag. The standard of William III was similar to that of James I, except that it bore at its center a shield displaying the arms of Nassau: a lion rampant, in gold, on a blue field strewn with gold billets or small vertical bars.

Until 1707 Queen Anne used the James I standard; but when England and Scotland, previously separate countries ruled by the same monarch, became the United Kingdom of Great Britain, this was symbolized by a new royal standard. The royal emblems of England and Scotland were impaled, with a slight modification, in the first and fourth quarters; the Harp of Ireland remained in the third quarter; but the Lilies of France were relegated to the second quarter, as though the English monarch's claim to the French throne were weakening.

Standard of William and Mary

THE PROPERTY OF
PALMERSTON AVE. PUBLIC
SCHOOL

Standard of Queen Anne, after 1707.   Standard of George I.

George I, who succeeded Anne in 1714, was Elector of Hanover and placed its arms in the fourth quarter. They combined those of Brunswick, two lions, gold on red; of Luneberg, a lion rampant, blue on a gold field strewn with red hearts; and of Westphalia, a horse, white on red. At its center, a shield displayed the Crown of Charlemagne, gold on red.

In 1801 Ireland was admitted into the Union, and a year later George III gave up all claim to the French throne. The Lilies of France were removed from his standard; the Lions of England occupied the first and fourth quarters; the Lion Rampant of Scotland, the second; and the Harp of Ireland, the third. The arms of Hanover appeared on a central shield surmounted by an electoral cap, which was later replaced by a crown.

Standard of George III.

57

As the Salic law, which precludes female heirs from inheriting a throne, prevailed in Hanover, that country separated from the British Crown at the accession of Queen Victoria in 1837, and its arms were removed from the royal standard.

This now quarters the Lions of England with the Lion Rampant and Tressure of Scotland and the Harp, which now symbolizes only Northern Ireland.

Personal flags of royalty

In 1960 Queen Elizabeth II adopted a new personal flag for use where the British symbolism of the royal standard would be inappropriate. Blue with a gold fringe, it displays in gold the letter 'E', with the royal crown above it, encircled by a chaplet of roses. It was first used when the Queen visited India in 1961. The same device on a field of the appropriate national arms also forms the Queen's personal flag when she visits certain countries within the Commonwealth.

As supreme head of the Royal Navy, in 1964 she resumed the title of Lord High Admiral, which had been in abeyance since 1827. The flag denoting this office, an anchor and cable in gold on a red field, is now worn, with the royal standard, by any vessel on which the Queen embarks.

When the Queen is embarked on the royal yacht *Britannia*, the ship wears (bow to stern) the Union Jack, Lord High Admiral's flag, Royal Standard, Union Flag, and White Ensign.

The personal standard of Prince Philip, Duke of Edinburgh, represents his descent from two royal families, the surname he adopted, and his title: it quarters the emblems of Denmark, three lions in blue on a gold field strewn with red hearts; of · Greece, a broad white cross on blue; of Mountbatten, two black pallets or vertical bars on white; and of Edinburgh, a black castle upon a rock, also on a white field.

(*Left*) personal flag of Elizabeth II, used in countries where the symbolism of her royal standard (*right*) would be inappropriate.

Personal flag of Prince Charles,
for use on his visits to Wales.

As a king's widow, Queen Elizabeth the Queen Mother impales the royal standard with her own arms. These quarter the Lion Rampant of Scotland with three longbows on ermine, all blue on silver. As her family name is Bowes-Lyon this is a good example of canting or punning heraldry.

Other members of the royal family also have personal standards, the royal standard distinguished in some way. The standard of a child of the British Sovereign bears a white 'label' with three points; a grandchild's label has five points. Some labels are distinguished by special emblems. Other royalty simply fly the royal standard, ermine-bordered.

The label on the standard of the Queen's eldest son bears no distinguishing emblem, but, as the Prince of Wales, Prince Charles's standard has at its center a shield bearing the Welsh arms ensigned with a prince's coronet. In 1968 the Queen approved a personal flag for the Prince's visits to Wales; it places on the principality's standard—the traditional arms quartering four lions, two red on gold and two gold on red—a small shield displaying the coronet of the Prince of Wales on a field of green, the official color of Wales.

Princess Margaret's personal standard has a label distinguished by a Tudor rose on the two outer points and a thistle on the central point. That of the Duke of Gloucester, the third son of George V, has a red St. George's Cross on the outer points and a red lion on the central point, and that of the Duke of Kent, the grandson of George V, has five points bearing alternately a blue anchor and a red cross.

60

Personal standard of the Duke of Edinburgh

Personal standard of the Queen Mother

Personal standard of the Prince of Wales.

The Union Jack

For centuries the patron saint of England has been St. George, and by 1277 his emblem, a red cross on a white field, had formed the country's national flag.

According to an ancient tradition St. Andrew was crucified, in A.D. 69, on a cross formed of two diagonal beams. Three hundred years later a monk carrying some of his relics was shipwrecked off the coast of Scotland, and for this reason a diagonal cross, white on a blue field, has long formed the Scottish emblem.

When James VI of Scotland became James I of England, he wished to represent both countries on his royal standard and on a combined national flag which all his subjects were to fly on their ships. Instructed to prepare a suitable emblem, his heralds placed the red St. George's Cross, bordered with white, on a field formed by the St. Andrew's emblem, to create the first Union Flag. This displeased the Scots, but the King was obdurate; however, he did order that though this new flag was to be worn at the maintop by all British ships, one or other of the older flags should also be worn in the foretop.

English flag of St. George

Scottish flag of St. Andrew

First Union Flag

Irish flag of St. Patrick.

Since 1801 the Union Flag of the United Kingdom has combined the national emblems of England, Scotland, and Ireland (now Northern Ireland).

After the Restoration, Charles II restricted the use of the Union Flag to royal vessels. In 1674, however, English merchantmen were allowed to fly a Red Ensign with the St. George's Cross in the canton, and at the Union of England with Scotland in 1707 this was replaced by a similar ensign with the first Union Flag in the canton.

When, in 1801, Ireland was admitted to the United Kingdom, it had to be represented on the Union Flag. The patron saint of Ireland is St. Patrick, and although the emblem chosen, a red cross on a white field, had nothing to do with him—it comes from the arms of a Welsh family long resident in Ireland—it has become known as 'St. Patrick's Cross'. Because the Scottish cross, as the senior, had to be given precedence, the Irish emblem was placed below it in the hoist and above it in the fly—the outer half of the flag—the crosses being counterchanged or reversed to make the right-hand arms of the red cross higher than the left-hand arms, and vice versa with the white cross.

In this way the present Union Flag was created, the emblem not only of the United Kingdom of Great Britain and Northern Ireland, but also of the British Commonwealth of Nations. Although the term 'Union Jack' is incorrect—it is only a jack when flown from the jackstaff of a ship—it is so generally used that to object to it would be pedantic.

White Cross of St. Andrew.

Red Dragon of Wales.

Trinacria of the Isle of Man.

Other national flags

England and Scotland are still represented by the Red Cross of St. George and the White Cross of St. Andrew.

The national flag of Wales is a red dragon displayed on a field of white and green, the principality's traditional colors. It commemorates the legend that in a vision Merlin saw a white dragon kill a red dragon which rose again, symbolizing the failure of the Saxons to conquer Wales. In 1953 Elizabeth II granted the flag an 'honorable augmentation', the dragon being surrounded by a scroll bearing the words *Y ddraig goch ddyry cychwyn,* 'The red dragon lends impetus'.

The larger Channel Islands have their own emblems. The flags of the lieutenant-governors of Jersey and Guernsey place at the center of the Union Flag a shield displaying three lions, gold on red; that of Guernsey is distinguished by a sprig of gold leaves. The St. George's Cross is hoisted over the official buildings of Alderney; at its center is a green, gold-bordered circle displaying, in gold, a lion rampant holding a sprig of green leaves. The seigneurial flag flown by the Dame of Sark is also a St. George's Cross; two lions, in gold, appear partly in the first quarter and partly in the right arm of the cross.

The island flag of Jersey bears the St. Patrick's Cross, a red cross on white. The state and island flag of Guernsey is a St. George's flag, but this may be flown only on land—at sea it is the distinguishing emblem of an admiral of the Royal Navy.

The flag of the Isle of Man bears an ancient emblem said to be of Sicilian origin, the *trinacria,* which represents three armed legs united at the thigh. The national flag of Man places it on a red field, that of the lieutenant-governor on the British Union Flag.

The historic symbol of Northern Ireland is the Red Hand of Ulster. It is based upon the legend that a chieftain deliberately severed his right hand and flung it ashore in order to establish his claim to rule the country by being the first in a race to touch it. Placed at the center of the St. George's Cross upon a white, six-pointed star ensigned with the royal crown, it forms the government flag of Northern Ireland, flown also by its citizens. A similar device on a white shield upon a gold circle surrounded by a wreath is placed at the center of the Union Flag flown by the governor.

Emblems of the Channel Islands:
(*right*) Jersey
(*below, left*) Guernsey
(*below, right*) Alderney

The White Ensign, which assumed its present form in 1801, has been the distinctive flag of the British Royal Navy since 1864.

The Royal Navy

For many centuries there was little to distinguish a British ship-of-war from a merchantman, except that a vessel engaged in war-like activities flew from her maintop a very long streamer or pendant. Individual ships were further distinguished by ensigns with the St. George's Cross in the canton, the fly being striped in colors chosen by their commanders.

Ensigns of red, white or blue were later used to distinguish between the three squadrons forming a fleet, the striped ensigns going out of use. In 1707 the St. George's Cross in the canton was replaced by the first Union Flag, and in 1801 this was superseded by the modern Union Flag; by this time the fly of the White Ensign was no longer plain but bore a large St. George's Cross.

The squadronal ensigns proved to be inconvenient and confusing, and during the Napoleonic Wars Admiral Nelson gave orders that in the presence of the enemy all vessels under his command should wear the White Ensign; the Union Flag was also to be flown from a foremast stay. These were the colors worn at the Battle of Trafalgar in 1805 when Nelson hoisted his famous signal: 'England expects that every man will do his duty'. In 1864 the squadronal colors were finally abolished, and the distinctive flag of the Royal Navy — though it is also flown by the Royal Yacht Squadron — became the White Ensign.

In 1924 George V approved the use by the Royal Navy, for ceremonial guards of honor, of a King's color. This—now the Queen's color—consists of the White Ensign charged at its center with a device including the royal crown and cypher. Following Army practice, the Royal Marines have both a Queen's and a regimental color. Each bears a device, the former at the center of the Union Flag and the latter upon the Blue Ensign; this includes a royal cypher ensigned with the royal crown, a terrestrial globe, and the motto *Per Mare, Per Terram*, 'By sea, by land'.

Except when it wears an admiral's or commodore's emblem, a ship of the Royal Navy is distinguished by the commission or masthead pendant, probably a survival of the ship-of-war's long pendant. The paying-off pendant, worn at the end of a vessel's commission, may be very long, depending on the amount of bunting that the signalmen have been able to 'acquire'. The church pendant is flown during divine service.

The badge of the Sea Cadet Corps, placed in the fly of the Blue Ensign, bears the Corps motto 'Ready Aye Ready', and represents a foul anchor, that is an anchor having a slack cable wound about it, ensigned by a naval crown.

The British Army

Until 1938 the British Army had no distinctive flag, but in that year George VI approved a badge for the Army, placing the royal crest, a lion standing upon a crown, before two crossed swords; on a red field this forms the Army flag.

By custom the masthead pendant (*top*) is lengthened at the end of a ship's commission to form the paying-off pendant (*bottom*).

The different regiments have always had their own distinctive colors, derived from the heraldic banners of the noblemen who had raised and commanded them. The colors are made of silk and elaborately embroidered, and the color pike on which they are carried is topped with the royal crest, the lion and the crown, in gilt metal.

As the senior cavalry regiments, the Household Cavalry and the Royal Scots Greys carry rectangular standards. Certain cavalry units carry not standards but guidons—from the French *guide-homme*, 'a guide to the men'—ending in a V-shaped fly with its corners rounded. The light cavalry units no longer carry drum banners swathing their drums; they are now used only by mounted squadrons of the Household Cavalry. Small pennons are attached to the lances used by the cavalry, but these are now carried only on ceremonial parades.

Infantry regiments carry two colors, the Queen's and the regimental. All colors, cavalry and infantry, indicate the actions in which the regiment distinguished itself, by names on scrolls or by special devices, such as a sphinx for Egypt, a dragon for China, and a tiger and elephant for India.

Queen's colors of the 3rd Battalion of the Coldstream Regiment of Foot Guards.

Today the cavalry carry their lances, bearing small flags called pennons, only on ceremonial occasions. But at the time of the Crimean War lances with pennons were carried into battle, and their purpose as a distinguishing emblem was partly decorative, partly functional. Here the 17th Lancers, one of the regiments in Lord Cardigan's ill-fated Light Brigade, charge the Russian gunners at the Battle of Balaclava on October 25, 1854.

Royal Air Force ensign.

Standard for an operational squadron of the Royal Air Force.

The Royal Air Force

The Royal Air Force, formed in 1918 by uniting the Royal Naval Air Service and the Royal Flying Corps, represents both in the colors of its ensign. This bears the Union Flag in the canton; its field of 'RAF blue' recalls the color of the sky, and in its fly are roundels of the national colors, the central red of the Army being separated by a white ring from the Royal Navy's dark blue.

The Royal Air Force color was approved by George VI in 1947 and resembles the ensign. The square field is fringed in silver and blue, with the royal cypher at the center.

There are also Queen's colors for certain units of the Royal Air Force; a silver wreath appears within their edges, and their centers bear a distinguishing emblem. That of the Royal Air Force College at Cranwell, for example, displays the figure of Daedalus who, according to Greek mythology, flew with a pair of artificial wings. The color of the Royal Air Force Regiment, formed during World War II to protect the airfields against attack, bears the royal cypher at its center and displays in its fly an astral or winged crown superimposed on two crossed rifles.

70

The standard for an operational squadron of the Royal Air Force is blue with a surrounding wreath of roses, thistles, shamrocks and leeks; the squadron badge appears at its center, and scrolls record its battle honors.

Formed in 1925 to identify enemy aircraft, the Royal Observer Corps places its own emblem, instead of the Air Force roundels, in the fly of the Royal Air Force ensign. Its central device, encircled with a wreath of laurel and surmounted by the royal crown, represents an Elizabethan coast-watcher holding up a torch, and it includes the motto 'Forewarned is Forearmed'.

The badge of the Air Training Corps, similarly placed in the fly of the Royal Air Force ensign, depicts a soaring falcon and places the Corps motto 'Venture Adventure' below it and an astral crown above.

The badge of the Ocean Weather Ships displays the Royal Air Force Eagle against the sun rising over the sea; this emblem, however, appears not on the Royal Air Force ensign but on the Blue Ensign.

Emblems worn on the RAF ensign:
(*above*) Royal Observer Corps
(*below*) Air Training Corps

Emblem worn on the Blue Ensign:
(*below*) Ocean Weather Ships

71

A governor-general's flag bears the royal crest with the appropriate country's name on a scroll.

The Queen's representatives

Members of the British Diplomatic Service have their own official emblems. Ambassadors and ministers abroad, ashore or afloat, fly the Union Flag charged at its center with a white circle displaying the royal arms. Consular officers when on shore also fly the Union Flag, but the central white circle displays a royal crown. When afloat, their flag is the Blue Ensign with the royal arms in the fly, although it is worn not as usual at the stern but at the bows of the vessel which carries them; the Red Ensign may fly at the stern.

A governor or lieutenant-governor of a country within the Commonwealth places the appropriate arms on a white circle surrounded by a garland at the center of the Union Flag. A similar emblem was formerly used by a governor-general, but this has now been replaced by a blue flag charged with the royal crest and bearing the Commonwealth country's name on a scroll.

The flag of a Queen's harbor-master is the Union Flag, but with a broad white border, and at its center the royal crown and the letters 'QHM' appear on a white circle.

The lord-lieutenant of a county flies the Union Flag with a central device which places the crown above a gold sword positioned horizontally and pointing towards the fly.

The Cinque Ports comprise several seaports which were once charged with important maritime duties along the southeast coast of England. The flag of the Lord Warden of the Cinque Ports — in recent times flown by Sir Winston Churchill and Sir Robert Menzies among others—is quartered, and displays three stylized representations of Dover Castle, a coronet and anchor, a sailing vessel at sea, six composite emblems of a lion and an ancient ship, and a larger representation of Dover Castle.

Trinity House is the principal pilotage authority in the United Kingdom and the general lighthouse authority, with responsibility for over six hundred buoys—in England, Wales, the Channel Islands and Gibraltar. It has several flags, all of which include a St. George's Cross in each of whose quarters appears a sailing ship on an 'heraldic sea' of wavy stripes, alternately blue and white.

Lord Warden of the Cinque Ports' flag.

Trinity House flag.

73

The Red Ensign, flag of the Merchant Navy
since 1801.

The pilot jack.

Flag 'H' of the
International Code.

The Merchant Navy

Except for those vessels which are authorized to fly the Blue
Ensign, the distinguishing flag of the Royal Naval Reserve, the
emblem of the Merchant Navy is the Red Ensign. As it is better
known in foreign waters than the Union Flag, it sometimes
appears in the flag books of other lands as the British national
emblem.

Like vessels of the Royal Navy, merchantmen used to fly
striped emblems as chosen by their masters. In 1674, as
already stated, their flag became the Red Ensign with the St.
George's Cross in the canton, this being replaced in 1707 by
the first of the Union Flags, and this again, in 1801, by the
present Union Flag, including St. Patrick's Cross.

Though on land the Union Flag is the British national
emblem, at sea its use is reserved exclusively for the Royal
Navy, whose vessels sometimes fly it on the jackstaff, that is
in the bows of the ship; it is then, and then only, that the flag
is correctly described as the 'Union Jack'. Merchantmen
may fly a Union Flag on the jackstaff with a broad white
border.

When hoisted to the masthead the same flag, sometimes

74

described as the 'pilot jack', is one of the signals used to summon a pilot. Alternatively he may be summoned by hoisting the flags of the International Code of Signals which indicate the letters 'PT' or 'G'.

To announce that a pilot is aboard, a vessel flies either a flag striped horizontally, white above red, or flag 'H' of the code, which is white in the hoist and red in the fly.

To warn passengers that she is about to sail, a vessel hoists the well-known 'Blue Peter'. This is the traditional name for flag 'P' of the International Code, a blue flag with a white oblong at its center.

Displaying, in red, a bugle ensigned with the royal crown and bearing the words 'Royal Mail' on a white field, the Royal Mail pennant shows that a vessel is carrying mail.

When in port in a foreign country a vessel may fly the flag of that country at her masthead; this 'courtesy flag' is intended to compliment her hosts. The correct emblem for Commonwealth or foreign vessels to use for this purpose in British waters is not the Union Flag but the Red Ensign.

The Blue Ensign, flag of the Royal Naval Reserve.

Flag 'P' or the Blue Peter.

Royal Mail pennant.

One of the earliest house flags, that of the Muscovy, or Russia Company which was incorporated in 1555.

The custom whereby merchant ships may indicate the shipping lines to which they belong by flying a house flag at the mainmast is of some antiquity, and in modern times it may be supplemented by a special device painted on the funnel.

The house flag of the Peninsular and Oriental Steam Navigation Company combines the colors of the royal houses of Spain, red and yellow, and Portugal, blue and white, in token of assistance rendered to members of both these families by vessels belonging to the line.

Adopted in 1968, the green and white flag of Canadian Pacific Steamships Limited bears a device combining a square to represent stability, a triangle to represent movement and a circle to represent global activity.

Like that of several other Scottish firms, the house flag of The Clan Line Steamers Limited displays the Lion Rampant of Scotland—though without the tressure which would convert it into a royal emblem. The jack of each of the line's steamers shows the tartan of the clan after which the vessel is named.

The Cunard Steamship Company Limited used to fly below its own house flag, displaying a lion rampant holding a globe, the pennant of the White Star Line, which has been amalgamated with it. The house flag of the Shaw Savill and Albion Company is like the former flag of New Zealand (page 56).

Shipbuilding companies may also use house flags, which they fly during a newly constructed vessel's trials. The house flag of Cammell Laird, which depicts a camel, is another amusing example of punning heraldry. When the vessel's owners are satisfied and take her over, this flag is lowered and their own house flag is raised.

Yacht flags

Vessels belonging to the members of certain yacht clubs are allowed to fly special ensigns. The Royal Yacht Squadron alone may wear the White Ensign; other clubs may use the Blue Ensign, with or without a distinguishing badge, and others may use the Red Ensign, similarly distinguished by a special badge. Apart from these, the flag of British yachts is that of the Merchant Navy, the Red Ensign.

Yachts may also fly a burgee or triangular flag from the top of the mainmast bearing their club's emblem, and a club's flag officer may fly, instead of the burgee, a rectangular or swallowtailed flag. Some yachtsmen also have their own 'house' flags. Other emblems are used to indicate that a yacht is racing or to denote the prizes she has won.

Cunard Steamship Company.

Peninsular and Oriental Steam Navigation Company.

The Clan Line Steamers.

Canadian Pacific Steamships.

Civil Air ensign.

British Airports Authority flag.

The Civil Air Services

Authorized in 1931, the Civil Air ensign bears the Union Flag in the canton of a flag of RAF blue with a dark blue cross of the St. George type bordered in white. It is flown over certain civil airfields and can also be hoisted over air transport buildings and by British aircraft when grounded.

The larger airports, however, are now flying the flag of the British Airports Authority. This is white and bears four oblique stripes—two red and two purple—which symbolize twin parallel runways.

Although large airports, which are busy at all hours, do not need to display any emblem to show that they are in operation, smaller airfields indicate this by the control tower flag, checkered in red and yellow.

Aircraft while in a foreign airfield, like vessels in a foreign harbor, may flag a courtesy flag, that of the country in which the airfield is situated; the appropriate emblem for foreign aircraft grounded in Britain is not the Civil Air ensign but the Union Flag.

The Royal Air Mail pennant, formerly used to denote the

conveyance of mail, has now been superseded by a device painted on the fuselage of the aircraft. It includes the words 'Royal Air Mail' and the traditional crown and post-horn.

The airlines have followed the example of the shipping lines by adopting house flags, flown above the airfields to which their aircraft fly as well as over their own buildings.

The house flag of British European Airways is white and is crossed by a broad red band bearing the corporation's initials; it also displays three astral crowns: crowns embellished with a device of stars and stylized wings.

The flag adopted by the British Overseas Airways Corporation is less ornate but equally effective: a 'speedbird' in gold on a gold-bordered blue burgee.

The only royal emblem to appear on the house flag of a British airline is that displayed by Caledonian Airways; this also depicts a winged lion symbol. The Red Dragon of Wales appears on the flag of Cambrian Airways.

Other house flags are that of British United Airways, which is crossed by two horizontal stripes—in blue and sandstone—and bears black lettering; and that of Autair International Airways, which is blue and displays in white a large letter 'A' and an outlined globe.

British European Airways house flag.

British Overseas Airways Corporation house flag.

Roald Amundsen and his companions, the first men to reach the South Pole, raise the Norwegian national flag on December 14, 1911 to mark the climax of their expedition.

Denmark: national and merchant flag.

Faroe Islands: national and merchant flag.

EUROPE

Scandinavia

Scandinavian flags have a general resemblance to those of Britain, although the vertical arms of the crosses they bear are not placed centrally on the flag, but somewhat nearer the hoist. Ensigns and government flags have swallow-tails.

The Danish national flag, which is also the merchant flag, is called the *Dannebrog* or 'Strength of Denmark', and is believed to be the oldest of the world's flags in continuous use. According to legend, in 1219 the Danish king Waldemar II and his troops were attacked in their camp while on an invasion of Estonia. They were about to be wiped out when the king saw a banner descend from the sky. He caught it and used it as a standard.

Norway was ruled by Denmark for 400 years until in 1814 it came under the Swedish crown. They retained the Danish flag, but added a lion arms in the upper corner. In 1821, because of the confusion with the Danish flag, the lion was eliminated and a blue cross covering most of the white cross of the Danish flag was added. In 1905 Norway became independent but retained the same flag. The ensign has three swallowtails and the jack is square; the royal standard places the royal arms on the ensign.

Norway: national and merchant flag.

Iceland: national and merchant flag.

Although part of Denmark, the Faroe Islands have their own national and merchant flag, which has been in use since 1931: a St. George's Cross edged with blue, red on white. Also part of Denmark, Greenland uses that country's flag. Although it has no flag of its own, it is represented on the royal arms of Denmark by a polar bear, white on blue; the Faroes are also represented — by a ram.

Iceland was ruled by Norway from 1262 to 1380 when both Iceland and Norway united with Denmark. It did not win complete independence until 1916 when it adopted its own emblem. The national and merchant flag places a red cross fimbriated with white on a blue field, an emblem which recalls the country's colonization by Norway, being the exact reverse of that country's flag. The government flag and ensign is swallow-tailed, as is the President's flag, which bears at its center the national arms; these include a bull, a vulture, a dragon and a giant, figures derived from an Icelandic saga.

Of the same pattern as the other Scandinavian emblems, the flag of Sweden is completely different from them in color, placing a gold cross on a light blue field. It dates from the sixteenth century but was readopted only in 1905 when the union of Sweden and Norway came to an end. The national and merchant flag is rectangular; the ensign, jack and royal standard have three swallowtails, the standard bearing the royal arms at the center of the cross.

The flag of Finland was adopted in 1917 when the country gained its independence from Russia. The colors on the flag are light blue and white, arranged in a cross to symbolize the country's waterways and snowfields and to denote its association with the other Scandinavian countries. Its merchant flag bears a light blue cross on a white field; its national flag places its arms on the intersection of the two arms of the cross. The ensign is a swallowtail of three points, and the President's flag adds an emblem in the canton.

Situated between Sweden and Finland are the Aland Islands. A semiautonomous part of Finland, in 1954 they adopted a flag which may be flown only on land. This combines emblems derived from its closest neighbors; the field is the light blue of Finland, but it otherwise resembles the Swedish flag, charged with a red cross.

Sweden: national and
merchant flag.

Finland: national flag.

Aland Islands: national flag.

Netherlands: national and merchant flag, and ensign.

Netherlands: jack.

Western Europe

The use of a tricolor, having three stripes, usually indicates that a country has won its freedom as the result of an armed revolution, a purpose for which this simple design is well suited. It would be difficult to produce a complicated flag like the Stars and Stripes or the Union Jack at short notice, or to disguise it without destroying it; but a tricolor can be rapidly stitched together, or unsewn even more rapidly, to produce three innocuous looking pieces of colored cloth.

When in 1579 the people of the Netherlands rose in revolt against their Spanish rulers, they adopted a flag based on the family colors of their leader, the Prince of Orange. It was originally a horizontal tricolor of orange, white and blue, but the orange stripe was replaced by a red one in 1650 to ensure greater visibility at sea. In this way the present national and merchant flag and ensign of the Netherlands was formed. On days of public rejoicing an orange pendant may be flown above the tricolor. The jack arranges the three colors in a distinctive pattern of twelve triangles, and the royal standard also differs completely from the national flag, bearing a blue cross on an orange field. Another well-known flag is that of the West Frisian Islands, a province of the Netherlands; its field is blue and crossed diagonally by three white stripes on which appear seven red hearts.

The national flag of Luxembourg was formerly identical with that of the Netherlands, but in 1890 the color of the lower stripe was changed to light blue. The standard of the Grand Duchess displays her arms, which quarter those of Nassau and Luxembourg, upon an orange field to show her family connection with the royal house of the Netherlands.

During their revolt against Austria in 1787–90, the Belgians chose colors derived from the ancient arms of Brabant. When they won independence from the Netherlands in 1830, these colors formed the national and merchant flag of Belgium, a vertical tricolor of black, yellow and red. The ensign places the colors as a cross on a white field, with two crossed cannon ensigned by a crown above the cross, and a foul anchor below.

Luxembourg national flag.

Belgium ensign.

Belgium: national and merchant flag.

One of the earliest French standards displayed three toads, in gold, on a blue field. In A.D. 496, however, King Clovis was inspired by a vision to convert them into three gold lilies, the heraldic *fleurs-de-lis*. Another early French flag was adapted from the coat of St. Martin, Bishop of Tours. Later this was replaced by the oriflamme, whose exact design is uncertain: it may have been blue or red, but it certainly ended in flame-like tongues. What flag Joan of Arc bore in her struggle against the English is still more uncertain; however, it must have displayed religious emblems as well as the *fleurs-de-lis*.

As already explained, the French royal standard originally displayed a number of gold lilies scattered over a blue field. In 1365, however, Charles V of France reduced their number to three and arranged them in a triangle. On some of the flags they appeared on a white field.

During the French Revolution the Republicans needed a flag, and they had an example to suggest its design—the red, white and blue tricolor of the Netherlands. This also had the

Legend tells that a vision inspired King Clovis to change the toads on his standard to lilies. Below, a more rational explanation.

86

advantage that it combined the colors of Paris, blue and red, with the white emblem of the French monarchy, the House of Bourbon.

France: standard of Charles V

The tricolor of France is distinguished from that of the Netherlands by having its stripes placed vertically, blue in the hoist, white and red. This forms the French national and merchant flag, ensign and jack, although vessels which served in the Free French Forces during World War II wear a blue and white jack, bearing the Cross of Lorraine on a white diamond. Officially the stripes are the same width but in fact they differ slightly, to make them look equal from a distance. The President's flag is normally square and bears his initials in gold on the central stripe.

France: national and merchant flag, ensign and jack.

In 1921 the Irish Free State adopted a vertical tricolor. Although based upon the French tricolor, it combines the green of Erin with the orange of the North, the central white stripes indicating the peace which should prevail between them. Its use was confirmed in 1937 under the articles of the new constitution, and it remained unchanged at the establishment of the Republic of Ireland (Eire) in 1949. The Irish

Eire: national and merchant flag, and ensign.

Germany: North German Confederation flag and later the merchant flag of the German Empire.

Harp, gold on a green field, which had once been the national flag of Ireland, now forms the jack of the republic; the President's flag places the gold harp on a blue field.

Until about a century ago Germany consisted of a number of separate states, and when the North German Confederation was formed in 1867, it united the black and white of Prussia with the red and white of the medieval Hanseatic League to form a tricolor of black, white and red.

The imperial standard of the German Empire, which was formed in 1871, displayed an eagle, and the naval ensign placed this at the center of a white flag bearing a black cross, with the black, white and red tricolor in the canton.

After World War I Germany became a republic, and the Weimar Convention decided that its federal flag should be striped horizontally, black, red and gold, but that the merchant flag should be the former black, white and red tricolor, with the federal flag in the upper hoist.

On attaining power in 1933, the Nazi party rejected the Weimar federal flag and restored the earlier black, white and red tricolor. At first with this, and then instead of it, the party used its own emblem: a red flag bearing a black swastika on a white circle at its center. The swastika is one of the world's most ancient and widespread symbols. It consists of a Greek cross with its arms bent at right angles, and it was adopted as the symbol of the 'Aryan race'. This flag went completely out of use at the end of World War II, being banned by order of the Allies.

After the war Germany was divided into two countries; both adopted the Weimar tricolor. This still remains the national and merchant flag of the West German Federal Republic; ending in swallowtails, it forms the ensign and jack. The government authorities flag displays on the tricolor a black eagle on a gold shield; this emblem, on a gold, red-bordered square, forms the President's flag.

The East German Democratic Republic also uses the black, red and gold tricolor, but distinguishes it by the gold emblem of a hammer and pair of compasses within a wreath. The state flag places this at the center of the tricolor, the merchant flag in the upper hoist. The naval ensign bears it at the center of a red flag crossed horizontally by the national colors, and the flag of the Head of State displays it upon a red, gold-edged field.

West Germany: national and merchant flag.

East Germany: state flag.

Central Europe

The Swiss flag displays a small equal-armed cross, white on a red field. The national flag is square, the merchant flag rectangular. Although not a tricolor, the Flag of Switzerland recalls the armed uprising against foreign rule by which the Swiss won their freedom. Gautier quotes the chronicler Justinger the Bearnois in explanation: in 1339 they chose as their emblem 'the sign of the Holy Cross . . . for the freeing of their nation was as sacred a cause as the deliverance of the Holy Places' in the Crusades.

The horizontal stripes of red, white and red on the national and merchant flag of Austria are taken from the arms of the Duke of Bebenberg, who during the twelfth century fought so furiously that his white surcoat was drenched with blood, except where his belt covered it.

The national flag of Liechtenstein is halved horizontally, blue over red, with a prince's crown in the upper hoist. The royal flag is similarly divided, gold over red.

The ensign and merchant flag of Hungary is a horizontal tricolor, red, white and green. The national flag displays at its center the country's arms, a shield in the same three colors flanked by two ears of corn.

Formerly divided between Germany, Russia and Austria, Poland regained its national identity, which it still retains, as a result of World War I. Its national flag is divided horizontally, white over red, and the merchant flag and the ensign display the country's arms in the center of the white stripe: a white eagle on a red shield. The jack places the arms in the center of a red-bordered white flag, and on the President's flag the eagle appears on a red field with an ornamental border.

Also formed as a result of World War I, Czechoslovakia unites two former provinces of Austria. In 1918 it combined the white and red of Bohemia, in two horizontal stripes in the fly; in 1920 the blue of Moravia appearing as a blue triangle in the hoist was added. The ensign of the armed forces adds in the upper hoist a red five-pointed star on which appears a white lion with a double tail. The President's flag places the national arms on a white field with an ornate red, white and blue border.

Switzerland: national
flag.

Austria: national and
merchant flag.

Hungary: national flag.

Poland: national flag.

Czechoslovakia: national
and merchant flag.

Liechtenstein: national
flag.

Spain: national flag and
ensign.

Andorra: one of the national
flags.

Southwestern Europe

The historic colors of Spain are the red and gold of Aragon;
although the republic formed in 1931 changed the lower stripe
of the Spanish tricolor to purple, the traditional color of
Castile. General Franco reverted to the former arrangement
when he came to power in 1939. The merchant flag of Spain
places a broad yellow stripe between two narrow horizontal
red stripes; the national flag and ensign displays the country's
arms toward the hoist. The jack quarters the emblems of
Castile, Leon, Aragon and Navarre. The red flag of the Head
of State is crossed by a yellow diagonal stripe, upon which the
heads of two 'wolf-dragons' appear, confronting one another.

For so small a country, Andorra, between France and Spain,
has a surprising variety of national flags. These combine the
colors of both neighboring countries in a tricolor, blue,
yellow and red, but this may be either vertical or horizontal
and may display either a coronet or a shield bearing the
country's arms.

Although the kingdom of Portugal became a republic in
1910, it retained its former arms but altered the national colors.
The new government at first wished to display the arms on a

Portugal: national and
merchant flag, and ensign.

Gibraltar: badge on the
British Blue Ensign.

red flag, but decided to add green in honor of Henry the Navigator.

The national and merchant flag and ensign of Portugal is green in the hoist and red in the fly. On the dividing line appears an armillary sphere, also in tribute to Henry the Navigator. Upon this a red shield displaying seven gold castles bears a smaller white shield on which appear five blue shields commemorating the victories which the first King of Portugal gained over five Moorish princes in the twelfth century; each shield bears five circles in reference to the five wounds of Christ, in whose name the victories were won. These arms also appear on the green-bordered red jack and on the green field of the President's flag.

To the south of Spain is Gibraltar, which was captured by a combined English and Dutch force in 1704, ceded to Great Britain in 1713 and is now part of the British Commonwealth. Its badge, which appears on the British Blue Ensign, symbolizes its strategic value as a fortress and as 'the key to the Mediterranean'; the Latin motto means 'The symbol of Mount Calpe'—the classical name of the Rock of Gibraltar.

Italy: national flag.

Monaco: national flag.

South-central Europe

For centuries Italy was divided into many small separate countries. Many wished for a united democratic government and were inspired by the revolution in France in 1789. In 1798 some students in Bologna led a revolution against their king. They changed the red, white and blue flag of France, substituting blue for green, a color which stands for nature and man's natural right to be free. In 1861 Victor Emmanuel II became king of Italy and added his coat of arms to the middle of the white stripe. In 1946 Italy became a republic and the coat of arms was removed. Although identical with the former merchant flag of Mexico, confusion was unlikely. The President simply uses the national flag.

The national flag of Monaco is the reverse of that of Poland. The Grimaldi family has ruled since the thirteenth century, and the flag's colors were taken from those in the family's coat of arms.

Since the fouth century San Marino, near Rimini, has been an independent republic; its national flag displays its arms — three towers, each topped by an ostrich feather — at the center of its merchant flag, which is halved horizontally , white over blue.

The dispute between Church and State in Italy ceased when, in 1929, Vatican City became completely independent. It is the only flag in Europe which does not follow the ancient rule of heraldry, placing white next to yellow (silver next to gold). The historic papal emblem in the center bears the triple crown and crossed keys.

The island flag of Malta once bore a Maltese cross, but this was replaced by a flag halved vertically, white in the hoist and red in the fly. For over a century, however, the island's national flag was the British Blue Ensign with a shield similarly divided in the fly. When George VI conferred the George Cross on Malta in 1942, that emblem was added in the upper right corner of both island flag and shield.

Malta, GC, became independent within the Commonwealth in 1964, and the former island flag then became its national flag, still displaying the George Cross. In 1965 it also adopted a merchant flag showing a white Maltese cross on a red field. Approved in 1967, the Queen's personal flag for Malta, GC, places Her Majesty's emblem upon the national flag.

San Marino: national flag.

Vatican City: state flag.

Malta, GC: national flag.

95

(*Above*) Yugoslavia: national and merchant flag.

(*Right*) Albania: national flag.

The Balkan Peninsula

Formed after World War I by uniting two independent states with regions from the former Austro-Hungarian Empire, Yugoslavia adopted a horizontal tricolor of blue, white and red, and when it became a federal people's republic in 1946 it added a red gold-edged star in the center. This is the country's national and merchant flag. The ensign places it in the canton of a red field, but here the star is surrounded by a golden wreath. The jack and fortress flag is red and displays the state arms at its center: five flaming torches below the red star. This device also appears in the tricolor canton of the red naval ceremonial flag.

Each of the republics forming the Socialist Federal Republic of Yugoslavia has its own flag: three use the same pattern as Yugoslavia itself, with differently arranged stripes, and two are red, one with the national flag in the canton, the other with the gold-edged red star in the upper hoist.

When Albania was freed from Turkish domination in 1912, the emblem it chose was the double-headed black eagle on a red background. This was the flag Skanderbeg used in the fifteenth century in his revolt against the Turks.

Rumania: national and merchant flag.

Bulgaria: national and merchant flag.

In 1944 a old-edged red star, the symbol of communism, was added to the national flag. The merchant flag places the star at the center of a flag striped horizontally, red, black and red.

The flag of the Socialist Republic of Rumania, which became independent in 1878, was originally a vertical tricolor of blue, yellow and red. When the country became the Rumanian People's Republic in 1947, its state emblem was added on the central stripe; it depicts an oil well towering among the trees in a mountain valley. The red star above it was added in 1952. This emblem also appears on the ensign, which is white except for a broad blue stripe along its lower edge, and at the center of the jack there is a gold-edged red cross on a blue field.

The Bulgarian national and merchant flag dates from 1878, the new national arms being added in 1947. It is striped horizontally, white, green and red. The arms appear in the upper hoist: a lion rampant in gold, with the red star above and a wheel below, flanked by ears of corn. The ensign places a red star on a white field with narrow stripes of green and red along its lower edge. The jack is red and bears a large red white-edged star at its center.

97

Greece has two national flags, and these form the basis of several other flags. That flown at sea, which is also the merchant flag, is striped alternately blue and white, its nine stripes being said to represent the number of syllables in the Green watchword *Eleutheria a thanatos,* 'Liberty or death'; in the square canton a white cross appears on a blue field. A gold crown in the center of the cross converts this flag into the ensign. The national flag flown on land consists simply of the white cross on the blue field. The square jack and the rectangular fort or service flag add the central crown. A 'target' of blue, white and blue at the center forms the Civil Air ensign, and if the crown is placed in the canton, the Air Force ensign. With the full arms of Greece at its center this flag becomes the royal standard.

Cyprus's former badge—two lions, in red, on a white circle—appeared in the fly of the British Blue Ensign. The country was ruled by Britain from 1878. On independence in 1960, Cyprus chose a white flag with a map of the island in gold above two green olive branches.

Against a frieze depicting an umpire and runners in the games of ancient Greece is one of the world's international flags, the flag of the modern Olympic Games. It was first raised in 1948.
(*Right*) Greece: merchant flag, and national flag at sea.
(*Below, right*) Greece: national flag on land.
(*Below, left*) Cyprus: national flag.

(*Above*) USSR: national and merchant flag.

(*Right*) USSR: ensign.

Russia and Turkey

When Russia was an empire, its merchant flag was striped horizontally, white, blue and red. The ensign displayed a blue cross on a white field, the reverse of the St. Andrew's flag. The Czar's imperial standard displayed a double-headed eagle.

The Bolshevist party made use of a traditional revolutionary emblem, the Red Flag. When, shortly after the collapse of the Czar's government in 1917, they came to power, it was natural that they should use this emblem, modified by a suitable device, as the flag of Soviet Russia. A British political son vividly expresses their mood in 'The Red Flag'.

> '*It reigned above our infant might*
> *When all around seemed dark as night;*
> *It witnessed many a deed and vow,*
> *We shall not change its colour now.*'

The national and merchant flag of the Union of Soviet Socialist Republics is thus the Red flag, with the state emblem in the upper hoist: a five-pointed star, outlined in gold, above a crossed hammer and sickle, also in gold, symbolizing the workers in industry and agriculture. The ensign of the Soviet Union is white, with a blue stripe along its lower edge, and displays the red star and the hammer and sickle emblem side by side. The jack places the white hammer and sickle at the center of a red star which is placed upon a larger white star, on a red field.

All the Soviet Socialist republics which constitute the Union have their own flags, most of which place horizontal stripes of various colors across the Russian national flag.

The national and merchant flag and ensign of Turkey is red, with a white crescent and star displayed in the hoist. In fact Turkey, once part of the great Ottoman Empire, still uses that empire's historic emblem. Legend tells that when Philip of Macedon—father of Alexander the Great—tried by a night attack to reduce Byzantium, later called Constantinople and now Istanbul, he was foiled by the brightness of the crescent moon. Becoming the symbol of the Byzantine Empire, it was later adopted by their Ottoman conquerors. The star was added about 1798. Some say it represents Thrace, a part of Turkey which lies in Europe.

USSR: jack.

The flag of a Soviety Socialist republic, Ukraine.

Turkey: national and merchant flag, and ensign.

Syria: national flag.

Jordan: national flag.

Iraq: national flag.

Bahrein: state or island flag.

ASIA

Western Asia

The Ottoman Empire once included most of the regions around the eastern end of the Mediterranean, and many of these countries still show the Moslem influence either by displaying the crescent moon and star symbol, or by using flags including the colors of the four historic Moslem families: black, white, green and red, for the Abbasids, Omyyads, Fatimids and Hashemites.

Placed by the League of Nations under a French mandate after World War I, Syria became a republic in 1941, and though from 1958 to 1961 it was associated with Egypt in forming the United Arab Republic, it never adopted that republic's flag. The Syrian national flag is striped horizontally, green, white, and black, with three red stars, standing for the Arab revolutions, on the central stripe.

The region once known as Transjordan was also freed from Turkish domination as a result of World War I. The national

Kuwait: national flag.　　Saudi Arabia: national flag.

flag of what is now the Hashemite Kingdom of Jordan is striped horizontally, black, white and green; in the hoist is a red triangle displaying a 7-pointed white star, representing the seven versions of the Koran. On a rectangular field of red, green, black and white stripes, the royal standard places a white rectangle bearing the national flag, with a gold crown instead of the white star.

The region once called Mesopotamia, the land 'between the rivers' of the Euphrates and Tigris, is now known as Iraq. Soon after the country became a republic in 1958 it adopted a flag striped vertically, black, white and green, with a golden circle on a large red star at its center. In 1963 this was superseded by the new national flag of Iraq; this is a horizontal tricolor of red, white and black and resembles that of the United Arab Republic, except that there are three, not two, green stars on the central stripe, indicating the close friendship that existed among Iraq, Syria and the United Arab Republic.

Bahrein, a group of islands in the Persian Gulf, flies a scarlet state or island flag which has along the hoist a broad white stripe with a zig-zag edge.

Since its independence in 1961, the state of Kuwait has used a flag consisting of three horizontal stripes, green, white and red, with a black trapezium in the hoist.

Although the flags of Saudi Arabia differ completely from those of the other Arab countries, they do not merely indicate but forcibly proclaim their Moslem origin. The national flag is green, bearing in white Arabic characters the declaration: 'There is no god but God, and Mohammed is the Prophet of God'; below this a sword appears, also in white. The merchant flag is triangular in shape, displaying, in white on green, two crossed swords, with a small foul anchor in the upper angle.

103

Yemen: national and merchant flag, and ensign.

Southern Yemen: national flag.

Lebanon: national flag.

The national and merchant flag and ensign of Yemen is a horizontal tricolor, red, white and black, with a five-pointed green star at its center: only the number of stars distinguish it from the United Arab Republic's flag.

Until recently the region in the south of the Arabian peninsula consisted of a number of Arab sheikdoms, some under the protection of the British, who also had a naval and air base at Aden. However, in 1967 the British withdrew, and the whole region became independent as the People's Republic of South Yemen. Its flag is striped horizontally, red, white and black, with a light blue triangle containing a red star in the hoist.

While under French mandate from the League of Nations, Lebanon flew the tricolor of France with its own emblem, the cedar tree, standing for strength, holiness and eternity, on the central stripe. When in 1944 it became an independent

104

republic, it adopted a new national flag, striped horizontally red, white and red. This retained the traditional 'Cedar of Lebanon' on the central stripe. In the hoist and fly of the jack is a white stripe displaying a red anchor.

When the country then known as Palestine was under British mandate from the League of Nations, its flag was the Blue Ensign with the word 'Palestine' on a white circle in the fly. Renamed Israel, it attained independence in 1948, and placed on its flag its colors, blue and white, and its emblem, the six-pointed 'Star of David'.

The national flag of Israel displays this emblem on a white flag between two horizontal blue stripes; the merchant flag places it in a white oval near the hoist of a blue flag; the ensign also shows it on a blue flag, in a white triangle at the hoist. The President's standard displays on a white-bordered blue flag another religious emblem, the seven-branched candle-abra, between two olive branches. Below is the word 'Israel' in Hebrew characters, the whole design being in white.

Israel: national flag.

Israel: merchant flag.

Israel: ensign.

Flags of the United Nations, Great Britain, Nepal and
India now fly on top of Mt. Everest since 1953.

Southern Asia

Most of the flags of Iran (Persia) are unusually long in propor-
tion to their breadth; formerly apple green, white and pink,
they adopted their present colors in 1933. The national and
merchant flag is a horizontal tricolor, now green, white and
red. The ensign and military flag displays upon its center the
national emblem: a lion brandishing a sword in front of the
rising sun, beneath a crown and surrounded by a wreath. This
emblem, without the crown and wreath, also appears on the
flag flown over government buildings. Until the nineteenth
century the lion was shown crouching. In 1834 the Shah
adopted the present flag, the emblem symbolizing power,
justice and purity.

When Afghanistan became independent in 1919, it retained
its former black flag, but in 1929 it adopted the traditional
Moslem colors. Its national flag displays a mosque between
two bunches of corn, in white, at the center of a vertical
tricolor, black, red and green.

The upper and lower portions of the double flag of Nepal

Iran: national and merchant flag.

Afghanistan: national flag.

Nepal: national flag.

107

India: national flag.

Ceylon: national flag.

bear stylized symbols of the crescent moon and the sun.

When the whole Indian subcontinent formed part of the British Empire, vessels of the Royal Indian Marine flew a Blue Ensign bearing the badge of the Star of India in the fly; they also wore a blue-bordered Union Jack at the bows and, when in commission, a red pendant.

In 1947 the subcontinent was divided into two separate areas, both of which remain within the British Commonwealth. The central region retained the name India and adopted a horizontal tricolor, deep saffron, white and bottle green, with a wheel emblem in dark blue at the center; this emblem, called the *Chakra*, symbolizes peaceful change. The ensign of the Indian Navy keeps the St. George's Cross, to symbolize its association with the other Commonwealth countries, with the national flag in the canton. The merchant flag places the national flag in the canton of a Red Ensign; the Indian Air Force ensign also places it in the canton, but the flag is RAF blue, with a target in the fly formed of concentric circles of saffron, white and green.

To the west and east of India are West and East Pakistan.

Pakistan: national flag
and ensign.

Maldive Islands: national
and merchant flag.

The national flag and ensign of the Islamic Republic is tartan green, with a broad white stripe down the hoist, and it displays the Moslem emblem, the crescent and star, in white. This flag forms the canton of the red merchant flag and the Pakistani Air Force ensign; the latter is RAF blue, and the target in the fly is green with a white center.

The former flag of Ceylon was the British Blue Ensign with a badge in the fly depicting an elephant in front of a Buddhist temple. On achieving a more liberal constitution in 1946, the island chose as its emblem the Lion flag of the former kings of Kandy. In 1950 the national flag of Ceylon added vertical bars of green and saffron in the hoist. This flag appears in the canton of the ensign, which is white with a St. George's Cross, and of the red merchant flag. The earlier Lion flag alone forms the canton of the Sinhalese Air Force ensign; again the fly is RAF blue, but the target, red with a gold center, bisects two horizontal stripes, saffron above green.

The national and merchant flag of the Maldive Islands displays the Moslem emblem, the crescent moon, white on a green rectangle at the center of a red flag.

109

Malaysia: national flag and jack.

Penang: state flag.

Sabah: state flag.

Southeast Asia

The Federation of Malaya, formed in 1950 to unite a number
of states and settlements, became independent within the
Commonwealth in 1957. Having been extended in 1963 to
include Sabah and Sarawak, on the north of the adjacent island
of Borneo, it was renamed the Federation of Malaysia. Although two years later the island of Singapore withdrew from
the Federation, which now consists of only thirteen states, the
national flag and jack of Malaysia still bears fourteen red and
white stripes, and the star which appears with the crescent
moon, gold on blue, in its canton still has fourteen points.
The naval ensign places this flag in the canton of a white flag
with a distinctive badge in the fly.

Each of the states which form the Federation has its own
flag. The crescent moon appears in gold on the blue canton of
the state flag of Malacca, which is halved horizontally, red
above white; and in white on that of Selangor, which is
quartered red and yellow; on a large red canton in the dark
blue flag of Johore; and in the center of the white-bordered
black rectangle which forms that of Trengganu. With its points
turned upward and the star above, the crescent moon appears,

with two lances and two swords, all in white on red, on the flag of Kelantan; and in green, with a yellow shield above and wreathed by two coconut leaves, on that of Kedah.

Two of the state flags are halved horizontally: that of Pahang, white over black, and that of Perlis, yellow over dark blue. The flag of Perak is striped horizontally, white, yellow and black.

The state flag of Negri Sembilan is yellow, with a canton halved diagonally, red over black. That of Penang is striped vertically, blue, white and yellow, with a palm tree depicted on the central stripe.

Of the two states on the island of Borneo, the flag of Sabah is striped horizontally, red, white, yellow and blue, and in the green canton Mount Kinabalu is silhouetted in brown, while the state flag of Sarawak is based on the arms of an historic figure famous in the region, Rajah Brooke of Sarawak: a crown appears at the center of a cross halved vertically, black and red, on a yellow field.

The British protected state of Brunei, although also in the north of Borneo, is not part of the Federation. A stripe, divided white above black, crosses its yellow flag diagonally, from the top of the hoist to the bottom of the fly; there is a central emblem of a winged pylon above a crescent facing upward between two hands, all in red, with a motto signifying 'Always render service through the guidance of God'.

Sarawak: state flag.

Brunei: state flag.

111

Singapore: national flag.

Although Singapore withdrew from the Federation, it kept its former state flag, which now forms its national flag; this is halved horizontally red over white, with the crescent moon, accompanied by five stars, all in white, near the hoist on the upper stripe. The naval ensign places this emblem in the red canton of a white flag with a large eight-pointed star in the fly. With the moon facing upward and surrounded by a circle, all in white on a red field, the same emblem forms the merchant flag.

While Burma was within the British Commonwealth, its badge, displayed in the fly of the Blue Ensign, depicted a peacock. When in 1948 it left the Commonwealth, it based its new flag on the emblem used by the resistance movement during the Japanese occupation. Its national flag is red, with a blue canton on which appears a large star surrounded by five smaller stars. The ensign places the blue canton with its stars in the canton of a white flag with a large St. George's Cross. The merchant flag resembles the national flag except that the entire upper half is blue.

Thailand (Siam), 'the country of the white elephant', at one time depicted that animal on a red flag. Annoyed, it is said, on realizing that an ignorant peasant had flown it upsidedown, in the 1920's, the King declared that he would have a flag whose correct position nobody should mistake; he chose to cross the red flag with horizontal white stripes, but later a central blue stripe was added. The national and merchant flag of Thailand therefore shows five horizontal stripes, but the ensign depicts the traditional white elephant on a red circle at its center.

The flag of the Mongolian People's Republic is striped vertically, red, blue and red; in the hoist an ancient magical emblem, the soyombo, is shown beneath a gold star.

Burma: national flag.

Thailand: national and merchant flag.

Mongolia: national flag.

Laos: national flag.

Cambodia: national and
merchant flag.

Indo-China, south of China, in the extreme southeast of Asia, was once ruled by France, and after it had been conquered by the Japanese during World War II, the French again tried to control that area. The flag of the French Resident was then a blue burgee, with the tricolor of France in the canton. In the 1950's, however, what had formerly been French Indo-China became three independent countries.

The red flag of Laos, independent since 1949, has the national emblem, a three-headed elephant under a parasol, symbolizing the three parts of the ancient kingdom united into one.

The national and merchant flag and ensign of Cambodia, which attained full independence in 1953, dates from A.D. 80. The steps of the triple-towered pagoda stand for the first five commandments of Buddhism. This represents the temple complex of Angkor Wat, probably the world's largest religious building, which fell into ruins after the capital Angkor had been attacked by the Chams in 1177.

Vietnam, a region including the former French protectorates of Annam and Tonkin and the colony of Cochin-China, was the third country formed from the dissolution of French Indo-China. In 1954 the Geneva Convention, in an attempt to end the war between France and the Vietminh, ordered the withdrawal of forces behind a line of demarcation, and Vietnam has remained divided into two zones ever since.

The flag originally adopted for all of Vietnam was yellow or orange, crossed horizontally by three narrow red stripes. It was retained by the southern zone, the Republic of Vietnam. The President's flag is golden-yellow, fringed in gold; at its center a bamboo tree is depicted in green, and below is a motto signifying 'Duty and Sacrifice'.

In 1955 the northern zones, the Democratic Republic of Vietnam, adopted a red flag with a large gold star at its center; as elsewhere, the color and emblem symbolize Communism.

In 1949 the region known as the Dutch East Indies attained independence as the Republic of the United States of Indonesia, and since 1963 it has included Western New Guinea (West Irian). The flag it adopted was that used by the nationalist movement. The jack is striped horizontally, five red stripes alternating with four white.

South Vietnam: national flag.

North Vietnam: national flag.

Indonesia: national and merchant flag, and ensign.

115

Communist China: national and merchant flag.

The Far East

China may have been the first country to use flags or banners, and some of these displayed a dragon—which in Chinese mythology is not a fearsome monster but a wise and benevolent counsellor. Some of the dragon flags also bore other emblems, and some had a field crossed with horizontal stripes. When the country became a republic in 1912, it abandoned the dragon emblem but retained the stripes; five in number and colored red, yellow, blue, white and black, these represented China's four provinces and its Moslem peoples.

The Nationalist government, set up in 1928, aimed at ruling the whole country, but it now holds only the island of Taiwan (Formosa); as it hopes to use this as a base for re-conquering the mainland, the Nationalist party naturally retains the emblem adopted in 1928. Hence the national flag and ensign of what is still called Nationalist China is red, with a blue canton dispalying a twelve-rayed sun in white. The field of the red merchant flag is crossed horizontally by four zig-zag yellow stripes; the jack is similar to the canton of the national flag. The President's flag is red bordered with yellow; the white twelve-rayed sun appears on a dark blue circle at its center.

The People's Republic of China, which now controls the whole of the mainland, uses the red flag of Communism. In upper hoist of the national and merchant flag appears one large gold star; four smaller stars nearby symbolize the cooperation of the republic's four social classes: the town workers, peasants, 'bourgeois', and 'patriotic capitalists'. The red flag of the Liberation Army of the republic places a star and three short bars in the upper hoist.

The island of Hong Kong, off the coast of China, was almost uninhabited until the British occupied it in 1841. Together with a small region on the mainland, it became a crown colony, and is still within the British Commonwealth.

It is represented by a badge on the Blue Ensign, and this formerly displayed a harbor scene, with a junk and a three-masted ship at anchor; on the wharf were shown two Chinese, one apparently greeting a white man is said to have represented a famous native guide.

In 1959, Hong Kong was granted a new coat of arms, which is represented in its entirety in a white circle in the fly of the Blue Ensign in place of the harbor scene. The shield displays a naval crown, gold on red, and below this two junks are shown upon the blue and white stripes which form the heraldic symbol for the sea; the crest depicts a lion holding a pearl, and the supporters are the British Lion and the Chinese Dragon. This badge surrounded by a wreath at the center of the British Union Flag forms the flag of the Governor of Hong Kong.

(*Above, left*) Nationalist China: national flag and ensign.

(*Above, right*) Nationalist China: merchant flag.

(*Right*) Hong Kong: badge on the British Blue Ensign.

117

Japan: national and
merchant flag, and jack.

Japan: ensign.

The national and merchant flag and jack of Japan, 'the Land of the Rising Sun', represents the country's traditional emblem by a red circle at the center of a white field. The ensign depicts the sun as emitting sixteen red rays and places it somewhat nearer the hoist. The Emperor's standard displays another of the country's emblems, a stylized chrysanthemum, in gold on a red field.

Long controlled by Japan, Korea obtained its freedom only when that country was defeated in 1945 at the end of World War II, but in 1950 it became the scene of a fierce civil war. In 1953, when the war ended, the region was divided into two separate nations.

At the end of the 1800's, when Korea came out of isolation and began to trade with other countries, she felt that she should have a national flag. From many designs submitted, the Emperor Kojong selected one with a white field, the color which stands for peace. The Koreans are particularly fond of white and are often referred to as "the White-clad People." The circle in the center is divided by an S-shaped line which means that there are two sides to everything, good and evil, male and female, night and day. The red half of the circle stands for the sun, the blue half for the moon. The bars are significant, too. Long bars outside short bars means the strong should support the weak. Short bars outside long bars mean that the most precious one should be protected by ones who are not as precious. Korea was seized as a colony of Japan in 1910 and was divided into two sections after World War II. The Republic of Korea (South) adopted the old flag, slightly changing the shapes of the red and blue areas and the position of the Divine Designs. North

118

Korea, the Democratic People's Republic, adopted a separate flag which included the five-point red star often seen in the flags of other Communist countries.

Formerly dominated by Spain, the Philippine Islands won their independence from that country, and immediately passed to the control of the United States in 1898. Though the country was allowed to fly its old revolutionary flag in 1920, this was with the proviso that it should be flown side by side with the Stars and Stripes and that the latter should be given precedence. In 1946 the Philippines obtained complete independence, and the American flag no longer had to be flown.

The national and merchant flag and ensign of the Philippines is halved horizontally, blue over red, with a white triangle in the hoist displaying, in gold, a sun and three stars. The jack also displays the sun and three-star emblem: the sun is displayed at the center of a blue field, and two of the stars appear in the upper and lower hoist, the third at the center of the fly. This emblem is based on the arms of Manila, the capital of the Philippines, and dates from 1596.

South Korea: national flag.

North Korea: national flag.

Philippine Islands: national and merchant flag and ensign.

Mauritania: national flag.

AFRICA

Northern Africa and the UAR

Moslem civilization spread from Arabia across North Africa, and several of the countries in this region, like those of the Middle East, show Moslem influence in their flags; in some by their colors, black, white, green or red, and in some by the emblem of the crescent moon and star. Later the whole area fell under the control of the peoples of western Europe, and it is only in fairly recent times that these countries have regained their independence.

Mauritania, a region in the extreme west of Africa, between the Spanish Sahara and Senegal, was occupied by the French during the early part of the twentieth century and later became a colony; it then formed part of French West Africa. On becoming independent of France in 1960, the Islamic Republic of Mauritania adopted a green flag displaying at its center the crescent moon with its horns upturned and the star above, both in gold.

When in 1956 the Kingdom of Morocco became independent it removed from the canton of its flag the small tricolor which showed that it had been a French protectorate. Later in the same year the former Spanish Morocco also gained its independence and was incorporated into the kingdom. Its flags went completely out of use; the merchant flag had been red, with a blue canton edged in white displaying the ancient mystical emblem known as 'Solomon's Seal'. The national and merchant flag of Morocco is now red, and its star takes the form of a pentagram, a mystical symbol.

The King of Morocco now uses the national flag. As Sultan, before 1956, he had flown a red pendant, bordered in yellow and displaying a yellow 'Solomon's Seal' bordered with green. The green flag of the Caliph of Spanish Morocco, which bore the same emblem, has also gone out of use.

Algeria, which had been annexed by France in 1842 and was regarded legally as neither a colony nor a protectorate but as part of Metropolitan France, won its independence only after fierce fighting, in 1962. Its national flag places the red Moslem Crescent and Star on a field halved vertically, green in the hoist and white in the fly.

Morocco: national and merchant flag.

Algeria: national flag.

Tunisia: national and merchant flag

Libya: national flag.

Tunisia, which had been a French protectorate since 1881, became independent in 1956. Its national and merchant flag places the crescent moon and star emblem, in red, upon a white circle at the center of its red flag. Before independence the Bey of Tunisia used a standard of very ornate design. It was striped horizontally, and the central stripe, which was twice as wide as the others, was green and displayed a white two-edged sword; the other eight stripes were alternately yellow and red and bore rowels of spurs alternating with crescent moons, all in colors contrasting with those of the stripes.

Freed from Italian rule by World War II, Libya was for a time placed under British and French administration by the United Nations, but the country became fully independent in 1951. Its national flag is a horizontal tricolor, the central stripe being broader than the others, and the colors of the stripes are said to represent the three regions which constitute the United Kingdom of Libya: red for Fezzan, black with the white crescent and star at its center for Cyrenaica and green for Tripolitania.

For centuries Egypt formed part of the Ottoman Empire and was ruled by Turkey. British troops were sent to the country to quell a revolution in 1882, and in 1914 a formal British protectorate was proclaimed over Egypt. This ended in 1922, but Britain and Egypt remained allies during World War II. In 1953 Ahmed Fuad II was deposed and Egypt became a republic. To denote its new status and its complete break with Turkey, Egypt adopted a new flag, completely different from the Turkish emblem: a green flag instead of red, and three white stars instead of one.

In 1958, Egypt, which by this time had become completely independent, formed the United Arab Republic in association with Syria, and although that country soon broke away, Egypt retained the name and flag of the United Arab Republic. Its national and merchant flag is a horizontal tricolor, red, white and black; two green five-pointed stars still appear on the center stripe. The ensign and jack places two crossed foul anchors in the upper hoist. The Air Force ensign places the national flag in the same position, and has a target on the fly: a white circle displaying two green stars separates the black center from the outermost red.

United Arab Republic: national and merchant flag.

Sudan: national flag.

Liberia: national and merchant flag, and ensign.

The Sudan, Liberia and Ethiopia

These three countries are being discussed separately for historical reasons, each having been in existence considerably longer than the recently formed emergent African states.

The Sudan had actually formed part of the domains of Egypt from about 2150 B.C. to 1580 B.C. and after periods of precarious independence it was again conquered by Egypt in A.D. 1801. Later, in 1899, it came under an Anglo-Egyptian condominium, and the flags of both those countries were flown on its official buildings. On becoming an independent republic in 1956 the Sudan adopted its own flag; this is striped horizontally, blue, yellow and green, representing the Nile, the desert, and the cultivated areas.

Liberia was not formed, so to speak, 'naturally'; it was founded in 1822 by the American Colonization Society as a refuge for the freed Negro slaves of the United States. It acknowledges its indebtedness to America by using a flag plainly derived from the Stars and Stripes. There is only one white star, however, in the small canton of the national and merchant flag and ensign of Liberia, since there was only one Negro republic in Africa at that time, and there are eleven red

124

Ethiopia: one of the national and merchant flags.

Ethiopia: obverse of the Emperor's standard.

and white stripes in the fly to commemorate the number of signatories to the country's declaration of independence.

Ethiopia (Abyssinia) is very ancient indeed; it is referred to in the second chapter of *Genesis* and by Homer, and Herodotus speaks of the 'blameless Ethiopians'. Its flag, which only dates from the end of the nineteenth century, may have begun as three colored pennants. The national and merchant flag of Ethiopia may be a simple horizontal tricolor of green, yellow and red, or it may bear the national emblem at its center: the 'Lion of Judah', crowned and bearing a cross. The ensign is blue, with the national flag in the canton.

The imperial standard of the Emperor of Ethiopia resembles the national flag but is fringed with gold and bears a special emblem, the Grand Cordon of the Seal of Solomon. This emblem surrounds devices and is surmounted by mottoes which differ on the flag's two sides. On the obverse it surrounds the 'Lion of Judah' emblem, and the motto signifies 'Conquering Lion of the Tribe of Judah'; on the reverse it encircles an illustration of St. George slaying the dragon, and the motto could be translated 'Strong Star of Honor'.

Mali: national flag.

Senegal: national flag.

Gambia: national flag.

Guinea: national flag.

Western Africa

The 'winds of change' which Harold Macmillan, the British statesman, described as blowing through Africa swept many of its countries free of European rule and made them independent—though some remain in the British Commonwealth, and others recall in their flags a former association with France.

Two adjoining countries—Mali, formerly the French Sudan, and Senegal, formerly part of French West Africa—show by the similarity of their flags that they were for a time associated as the Federation of Mali. These are both vertical tricolors, green, yellow and red, but whereas that of Mali bears no distinguishing emblem—the stylized representation of a Negro dancer having been removed from the yellow stripe—that of Senegal displays a green five-pointed star at its center. Both became independent in 1960, and Senegal is still a member of the French Community.

Gambia was represented on the British Blue Ensign by a badge depicting an elephant in front of a palm tree, but on attaining independence within the Commonwealth in 1965 it

126

THE PROPERTY OF

PALMERSTON AVE. PUBLIC
SCHOOL

Book No.

adopted a flag striped horizontally red, blue and dark green, with narrower stripes of white between the colors.

The flag of Guinea is similar to those of Mali and Senegal, except that its colors are reversed: it is striped vertically, red, yellow and green. This country was also part of French West Africa but gained its independence in 1958.

Sierra Leone was founded late in the eighteenth century to secure a home for freed Negro slaves and homeless Negroes from Britain. On becoming independent within the Commonwealth in 1961, it adopted a flag striped horizontally, green, white and blue. The Queen's personal flag for Sierra Leone, approved in 1961, places the royal emblem on a field resembling the country's arms; the lion under three lighted torches and a stylized mountain range, or *sierra,* make the arms an example of punning heraldry.

The Ivory Coast, independent of France since 1960, flies a vertical tricolor, orange, white and green.

Upper Volta retained its old name when it obtained full independence from the French in 1960. Its flag is striped horizontally, black, white and red.

Sierra Leone: national flag.

Ivory Coast: national flag.

Upper Volta: national flag.

Ghana: national flag.

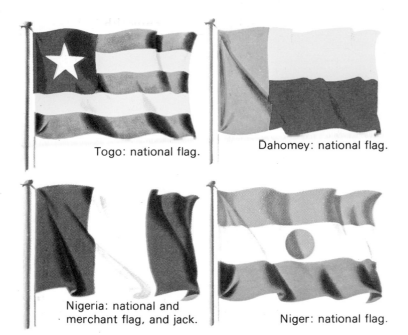

Togo: national flag.

Dahomey: national flag.

Nigeria: national and
merchant flag, and jack.

Niger: national flag.

The region formerly known as the Gold Coast was indicated on the British Blue Ensign by a badge similar to that of Gambia, but bearing the letters 'GC' instead of 'G'. In 1957 it became independent within the Commonwealth as Ghana, and adopted as its national flag a horizontal tricolor of red, yellow and green, with a large black star at its center.

When World War I broke out in 1914, the Germans surrendered their colony of Togoland to Britain and France. The British portion became part of what is now Ghana, while the French administered the part adjoining their own colony Dahomey, then within French West Africa. The national flag of the Republic of Togo—its name since it became independent in 1960—bears five horizontal stripes, three green and two yellow, and its red canton displays a white star.

Dahomey itself gained full independence in 1960. Its flag has a vertical green stripe in the hoist and two horizontal stripes, yellow over red, in the fly.

The former badge of Nigeria, in the fly of the British Blue Ensign, was a red circle showing the royal crown on a device of interlaced equilateral triangles, in green. Independent in

1960, and a republic within the Commonwealth in 1963, the country has a national and merchant flag and jack striped vertically, green, white and green; the ensign places the national flag in the canton of a St. George's Cross.

Niger, a territory of French West Africa and later for a time a member of the French Community, gained full independence in 1960. Its flag is a horizontal tricolor, orange, white and green, with a small orange circle at its center.

Central and Eastern Africa

During World War I the German colony of Kamerun was conquered by British and French troops, and it was divided later into a British and a French sphere of influence. Part of the British region was united to Nigeria, and the remainder, with the French region, became independent as the Cameroon Republic in 1961. Its flag is striped vertically, green, red and yellow, with two gold stars in the upper hoist.

The region formerly known as Spanish Guinea became independent in 1958 as Equatorial Guinea. Its flag bears three

Cameroon: national flag

Chad: national flag.

Central African Republic: national flag.

Congo (Brazzaville): national flag.

horizontal stripes, green, white and yellow, with a blue triangle in the hoist; a central shield, in gold, displays a silk-cotton tree and is placed below six gold stars and above a motto in Spanish signifying 'Unity, Peace, Justice'.

What was French Equatorial Africa was divided in 1960 into four independent states, all of which are members of the French Community. The flag of Chad has three vertical stripes, blue, yellow and red.

That of the Central African Republic is striped horizontally, blue, white, green and yellow, with a vertical red stripe at its center and a gold star at the top of the hoist.

The flag of the Republic of Congo or Congo (Brazzaville), formerly the Middle Congo, is green in the upper hoist and red in the lower fly, the two colors being separated by a broad yellow stripe crossing the flag diagonally from the bottom of the hoist to the top of the fly.

The national flag of the Republic of Gabon is a horizontal tricolor of green, yellow and blue.

The Somali Republic (Somalia) consists of the territories

Red Cross hospitals, vehicles and helpers bear an emblem which symbolizes their purpose: the impartial relief of suffering.

Gabon: national flag.

Somalia: national flag.

once known as British Somaliland and Italian Somaliland. The former was represented by a badge in the fly of the British ensigns. It depicted a shield displaying native weapons, a ninaret, a dhow at sea and an anchor; the crest was a kudu's head surmounted by a royal crown. On gaining independence in 1960 the two regions combined, retaining the emblem of Italian Somaliland as their national flag: a white five-pointed star at the center of a blue field.

The region known as the Congolese Republic or Congo (Kinshasa) became independent in 1960; hitherto the Belgian Congo, it had had its own flag, displaying a gold star on a blue field. In spite of its complete break with Belgium, it still places

Congolese Republic: national flag.   Rwanda: national flag.

Burundi: national flag.   Uganda: national flag.

this emblem on its national flag, but the star now appears in the upper hoist, and the field is crossed diagonally from the bottom of the hoist to the top of the fly by a red stripe edged with yellow.

A small area to the east of the former Belgian Congo, Ruanda-Urundi, was originally part of German East Africa, but as a result of World War I was administered by Belgium, first under a mandate from the League of Nations and later as a United Nations trust territory. In 1962 Rwanda became an independent republic. Its national flag is a vertical tricolor, red, green and yellow, with a large letter 'R' on the central stripe.

That of the Republic of Burundi, also independent since 1962, bears a white cross with red above and below the center and green in the hoist and fly; on a central white circle are three green-bordered, red six-pointed stars.

A number of regions in central and southern Africa are independent within the Commonwealth; most were formerly represented by badges on the British Blue Ensign but now have their own national flags.

When Uganda became independent in 1962, it retained its badge, displaying a crested crane, but placed this at the center of a flag striped horizontally in black, yellow and red.

On gaining its independence in 1963, Kenya abandoned its former badge of a lion rampant and adopted a flag striped horizontally black, red and green, with narrow white stripes between these colors; an African shield upon two crossed assegais, or native spears, is depicted at its center.

The German colony of Tanganyika became a British mandate after World War I, and was symbolized by the head of a giraffe. The flag of Zanzibar was red, but the British Resident placed on the ensign a badge showing an Arab dhow. Both symbolized their independence by adopting new flags. In 1964 they joined to form the United Republic of Tanzania. Their national flag is green in the upper hoist and blue in the lower fly, and is crossed diagonally from the base of the hoist to the top of the fly by a black stripe edged with gold.

In 1953, three regions within the Commonwealth united to form the Federation of

Kenya: national flag.

Tanzania: national flag.

Malawi: national flag.

Zambia: national flag.

133

Rhodesia and Nyasaland, represented by a badge displaying symbols taken from their respective arms. Ten years later, however, the Federation dissolved, its members still remaining within the Commonwealth.

The former Nyasaland, now renamed Malawi, uses a flag striped horizontally, black bearing a rising sun emblem in red, red and green. Zambia, formerly Northern Rhodesia, flies a green flag; in the upper part of the fly an eagle appears, and in the lower part three vertical stripes, red, black and orange.

Southern Rhodesia then became Rhodesia and flew a British ensign—its blue field lighter than usual—with a badge showing a miner's pick and above, a red lion between two thistles. In 1968 Rhodesia adopted a new flag striped vertically, green, white and green. At its center appear the national arms: the shield displays the emblems which appeared on the British ensign; the supporters are sable antelopes, and the crest, in gold, is one of the Zimbabwe birds, soapstone figurines discovered in the ruined city of Zimbabwe. The motto might be translated 'May it be worthy of the name'.

Rhodesia: national flag.

Malagasy: national flag.

Botswana: national flag.

Lesotho: national flag.

134

Some African islands

Madagascar was under French rule but became independent as the Malagasy Republic in 1960, while remaining within the French Community. Its flag has a broad white stripe in the hoist and two stripes, red above green, in the fly.

Some smaller African islands, being within the Commonwealth, are represented by badges on the Blue Ensign; that of St. Helena shows an Indiaman about to sail between two cliffs, that of the Seychelles a beach scene. Mauritius formerly used its arms as a badge but since independence has flown a new flag striped horizontally, red, blue, yellow and green.

Three states in Southern Africa

Three states in the southern part of Africa now have new flags: Botswana (formerly Bechuanaland), a blue flag crossed horizontally by a black stripe edged with white; Lesotho (formerly Basutoland), a blue flag with vertical stripes of green and red

Mauritius: badge on the British Blue Ensign, now replaced by a national flag.

Seychelles: badge on the British Blue Ensign.

St. Helena: badge on the British Blue Ensign.

135

in the hoist and with a native hat depicted in the fly; and
finally Swaziland, a flag on which two horizontal blue stripes
are separated by a broader red stripe edged with yellow and
displaying, in black and white, an African shield and spears.

Republic of South Africa

Cape Colony was settled by the British and by the *Boers*
(farmers) from Holland, but friction between the two races
induced the latter to set out in 1835–36 on their Great Trek
northward to found Natal, the Orange Free State, and the
Transvaal.

In 1839 they founded the Republic Natalia; until this became British in 1843 it flew an adapted Dutch flag in which the
central stripe became a white triangle extending from the fly
to the midpoint of the hoist. William III of Holland designed
a flag for the Orange Free State to symbolize the relationship
between the two countries; its white field was crossed horizontally by three orange stripes, and it bore the Dutch flag in the
canton. The Transvaal adopted the *vierkleur* (four colors) flag,
consisting of the Dutch tricolor of red, white and blue, with a
broad green stripe, to represent 'Young Holland', extending
down the hoist.

After the Boer War of 1899–1902 the four regions were
united as South Africa, and their emblems combined in a badge
on the Red and Blue Ensigns: a white-robed female figure
grasping an anchor for the Cape of Good Hope; two wild oxen
for Natal; an orange tree for what was now the Orange River
Colony; and a trek wagon to represent the Transvaal.

When in 1926 the Union of South Africa gained dominion
status, it adopted a new national flag, retaining this when it
withdrew from the Commonwealth to become a republic in
1961. The national flag of the Republic of South Africa is a
horizontal tricolor, orange, white and blue, with three small
flags displayed on the central stripe: the old Orange Free State
flag, the British Union Jack and the old *vierkleur* or four-color
flag. This is also the merchant flag and the jack; the ensign
places it in the canton of a white flag with a broad green cross.
The ensign of the South African Air Force is light blue with a
badge in the fly superimposing a leaping springbok on a
stylized plan of the historic fort at Cape Town; the canton is
the national flag.

National and merchant flag and jack of
South Africa.

Ensign of South Africa.

Air Force ensign of South Africa.

AUSTRALASIA

Australia

The national flag of Australia, which has been flown since the beginning of the century, consists of the British Blue Ensign distinguished by a regional emblem. Beneath the Union Flag in the canton appears a large seven-pointed 'Commonwealth Star', and in the fly are five smaller stars, representing the constellation of the Southern Cross. All these stars are white, and, placed in the same way upon the Red Ensign, they form Australia's merchant flag.

The Queen's personal flag for Australia was approved in 1962. It places the royal emblem upon a field displaying the

National flag of Australia. | Elizabeth II's personal flag for Australia.

arms of the Commonwealth of Australia, which combine the emblems of its six states.

Having always worn the British White Ensign, the Royal Australian Navy adopted its own White Ensign in 1967. This still bears the Union Flag in the canton, but the St. George's Cross has been replaced by stars similar to those on the national flag, except that they are blue on a white field.

The ensigns of the Royal Australian Air Force and the Australian Civil Air Service adapt the symbols on the national flag to harmonize with the corresponding British ensigns.

White Ensign of the Royal Australian Navy.

Royal Australian Air Force ensign.

Australian Civil Air ensign.

Destruction of the Emden by the HMAS *Sydney* in World War I.

139

Each of the six states which form the Commonwealth of Australia has its own coat of arms, and these emblems, suitably adapted, are displayed in the fly of the British Blue Ensign hoisted over state government buildings.

The badge of Western Australia represents the black swan, which is indigenous to this region, on a yellow circle.

That of South Australia also depicts a native bird, the white-backed piping shrike, again upon a yellow circle.

The badge of Queensland displays the royal crown at the center of a Maltese cross, shown in blue on a white circle.

New South Wales uses as its badge the St. George's Cross, red on a white circle; at its center appears a lion, and on each of its arms a star, all in gold.

The island of Tasmania also displays the Lion of England, in red, on a white circle.

Victoria, then of course a colony and the first in Australia to have its own warship, H.M.S. *Nelson*, was likewise the first to have its own flag, in 1886; it displayed the Southern Cross in the fly of the Blue Ensign, the royal crown being added about seven years later.

The Southern Cross has been regarded as a suitable emblem for Australia—and for New Zealand—for over a century. According to Frank Cayley's admirable book *Flag of Stars*, a flag somewhat similar to the present badge of New South Wales was suggested in the early 1820's: 'That first "flag of stars" in Australia's history was a white flag charged with the Red Cross of St. George, having in each corner a star to symbolize the Southern Hemisphere under the constellation of the Southern Cross.'

Although this flag was never popular, it influenced several later designs, including ensigns on which the British Union Flag was placed in the canton of a variety of fields: the St. George's Cross bearing five stars on its arms and center and a number of horizontal blue and white stripes symbolizing the oceans between Australia and Great Britain; a white field bearing a blue cross of the St. George type, with the usual five white stars; and a leaping kangaroo.

As a result of a public competition held in 1901, the present Southern Cross design was chosen, and this was approved by Edward VII in 1903 as the national flag of Australia.

Western Australia

South Australia

Queensland

New South Wales

Tasmania

Victoria

Each state in the Commonwealth of Australia has a badge adapted from the state arms. These are placed in the fly of the British Blue Ensign which is flown over state government buildings.

National flag of New Zealand.

United Tribes of
New Zealand flag.

White Ensign of the Royal New
Zealand Navy.

New Zealand

The national flag of New Zealand, like that of Australia, places the Southern Cross emblem in the fly of the British Blue Ensign but represents it differently: only four stars are shown instead of five, and they are not white but red with a white fimbriation. The four stars are also shown on the merchant flag, but here they are depicted in white.

The Queen's personal flag for New Zealand, like that for Australia, was authorized in 1962, and places Her Majesty's emblem on a field formed by New Zealand's arms. They combine the Southern Cross with symbols of the nation's commerce and of its animal, vegetable and mineral wealth: two heraldic ships, a fleece, a wheatsheaf and mining tools.

In 1968 the Royal New Zealand Navy, which had previously worn the British White Ensign, replaced this by its own White Ensign, with the Union Flag in the canton and the Southern Cross, represented by four red stars, in the fly; the jack is formed by the New Zealand national flag. The ensign of the

Royal New Zealand Air Force places the letters 'NZ' in white at the center of a target similar to that on the British Royal Air Force ensign; the New Zealand Civil Air ensign places the stars of the Southern Cross in the fourth quarter of the corresponding British ensign.

According to Frank Cayley's *Flag of Stars,* the present New Zealand flag had several unofficial forerunners. The necessity for such a flag was made clear when in 1830 a New Zealand vessel was seized by the customs authorities at Sydney for not flying any flag. As the region had not yet become a colony, ships built in its yards could not sail under British register.

A few years later the newly appointed British Resident in New Zealand asked the authorities in Sydney to design a suitable flag. However, the result—four horizontal blue stripes on a white field, with the Union Jack in the canton—disappointed him for it contained so little of the color red which the Maoris associate with rank.

He, therefore, had three designs voted for by the white settlers and the Maoris. The one chosen was a St. George's Cross

The field of Elizabeth II's personal flag for New Zealand (*left*) shows emblems of the country's wealth and commerce, as well as the Southern Cross.

(*Below, left*) Royal New Zealand Air Force ensign.

(*below, right*) Royal New Zealand Civil Air ensign.

The Western Pacific High Commissioner's emblem is centered on the British Union Flag.

These arms, in the fly of the British Blue Ensign, represent the British Solomon Islands.

The New Hebrides place their badge in the fly of the British Blue Ensign.

having in the canton a smaller red cross fimbriated with white on a blue field, with a white star in each quarter.

This flag of the United Tribes of New Zealand was flown for only a few years. Then it was replaced by the British Union Flag and became the house flag of Shaw Savill and Albion Company Limited. For a time the Union Flag was superseded by the British Blue Ensign with the letters 'NZ' in the fly, and the present flag was approved in 1902.

The Pacific

A number of islands and archipelagos in the Pacific Ocean—including the British Solomon Islands, the Gilbert and Ellice Islands, the New Hebrides and the Phoenix Islands—come under the jurisdiction of the Western Pacific High Commissioner. His emblem is the British Union Flag, bearing at its center a white circle on which the letters 'WPHC' appear, ensigned with the royal crown and surrounded by a garland. Some of these groups of islands, however, also have their own flag.

The British Solomon Is-

Guam: Governor's flag.

lands Protectorate, for example, put its arms in the fly of the
Blue Ensign. They take the shield, on whose upper part the
Lion of England appears, gold on red, and whose lower part
depicts an eagle, a turtle, native weapons and two frigate
birds on a field quartered blue and white.

The New Hebrides, a group of islands in the southern
Pacific, form a condominium, administered jointly by Britain
and France. Their badge, flown within a garland at the center
of the British Union Flag and without a garland on the Blue
Ensign, shows on a white disc a royal crown with the words
'New Hebrides' in black.

Papua and New Guinea, being administered by the Australian government, use the Blue and Red Ensigns with the Commonwealth Star and the Southern Cross that form the national
and merchant flags of Australia.

The island of Guam was formerly Spanish, but toward the
end of the nineteenth century it was ceded to the United States,
by whom it is used as an air and naval outpost. The seal of the
Governor of Guam appears at the center of a blue flag; it
depicts an island scene, including an outrigger canoe.

Nauru, a small island annexed by the Germans in 1888, was
taken over by Australia in 1914, and except for a period during
World War II was administered by that country under a
League of Nations mandate and later under a United Nations
trusteeship agreement. In 1968 it became independent
and now has its own flag. The blue field represents the Pacific
Ocean and the sky; the gold horizontal stripe and the white star
symbolize Nauru's position immediately south of the equator.

The Tongan or Friendly Islands form a monarchy within the
Commonwealth. The King of Tonga's standard is quartered

and displays three stars, a crown, a dove bearing an olive branch in its beak and three piled swords; at its center a red Greek cross appears on a white star. The red cross also appears in the white canton of the red Tongan state flag.

The Fijian Islands place their full coat of arms on the Blue Ensign. A lion holding a coconut in its paws is shown, gold on red, in the upper part of the shield; the lower part is quartered by a St. George's Cross and displays three sugar canes, a coconut palm, a dove carrying an olive branch in its beak and a bunch of bananas; the supporters are Fijians, and the crest is a Fijian canoe. The motto *Rere vaka na kalou ka doka na tui* means 'Fear God and honor the king'.

The badge of the Gilbert and Ellice Islands depicts the sun rising over the sea, above which a frigate bird is flying; it is placed on the Blue Ensign.

Samoa, called by the French Navigators' Islands, consists of two groups of islands and islets. Those of Western Samoa were for a time under German rule but were taken over in 1914 by a New Zealand expeditionary force and remained under that country's rule until 1962, when they became the

Tonga: royal standard.   Tonga: state flag.

Western Samoa: national and merchant flag.

Gilbert and Ellice Islands: badge on the British Blue Ensign.

Former badge of Western Samoa, replaced by the flag opposite.

first independent Polynesian state. Formerly represented by a badge on the British Blue Ensign showing a beach scene including three coconut palms, Western Samoa now has its own national and merchant flag — red, except for a blue canton, upon which the Southern Cross appears as five white stars.

The flag of American Samoa is blue, with a white red-bordered triangle extending from the fly to the hoist. Upon the triangle is shown a flying eagle in natural colors, holding in its talons two traditional Samoan emblems, denoting wisdom and power.

Some conclusions

Thus, the smallest and most remote islands of the southern seas, like the great land masses of the north, represent their national indentity and ideals by the time-honored method of flying a flag bearing emblems of local significance.

Throughout the world the history of the various regions is symbolized by their flags. A brief comparison with flag books published earlier this century shows how greatly conditions have altered in a lifetime. Gone are many of the ensigns which distinguished colonies in the British Empire; gone too are flags implying French, Belgian or Dutch rule. They have been replaced by emblems showing that these countries, although perhaps still associated with their former rulers, are now independent sovereign states. Moreover, there are two regions whose history and use of flags has only recently begun.

The coat of arms assigned to the British Antarctic Territory.

ANTARCTICA

A number of explorers have flown their national flags over the Antarctic, and the Stars and Stripes and United Nations flag were hoisted over the Amundsen-Scott South Pole Station to inaugurate the International Geophysical Year (1957–58).

In 1962 a separate colony, the British Antarctic Territory, was formed from the South Shetlands, South Orkneys and Graham Land. It was given the arms of the former Falkland Island dependencies. On a white shield are wavy blue lines, to represent snowfields and the Antarctic Ocean, and a gold torch, the symbol of knowledge, on a red triangle. The supporters suggest Britain and Antarctica, a lion and an emperor penguin; the motto is 'Research and Discovery', and the crest displays an explorer's vessel.

In 1965 the Australian National Antarctic Research Expedition adopted a pendant, to be flown beside the Australian national flag at all their bases in Antarctica. On a green field a gold leopard seal is outlined in black, and below, the letters 'ANARE' appear above a golden boomerang.

FLAGS IN SPACE

Flags have now been taken not only to the ends of the earth but out into space.

The Russian spacecraft *Luna 1,* which in January 1959 attempted to reach the moon, carried a metal 'pendant' engraved with the name of the Soviet Union. *Luna 2,* which reached the moon on September 13, 1959, scattered over its surface a number of tiny Russian flags.

Luna 9, which landed on the moon in February 1966, carried a pendant bearing the words 'Union of the Soviet Socialist Republics' in the Cyrillic alphabet as well as symbols of the earth, the moon, and the spacecraft's path.

The American astronauts who 'walked in space' displayed their country's flag on the sleeve of their spacesuits and released a larger flag beyond the atmosphere. The American flag was also sent to the moon in June 1966 sealed inside the tubing of the space capsule, *Surveyor 1.*

On July 20, 1969 the Stars and Stripes, wired to stand out firmly in the absence of air, was planted on the moon by American astronauts Neil A. Armstrong and Edwin E. Aldrin.

SIGNAL FLAGS

Signals have been given from time immemorial, but perhaps not very systematically; Greek and Roman literature refers only to the raising or waving of a brightly colored cloak. The earliest code of naval signals appears to have been drawn up in the ninth century by the Byzantine Emperor Leo V, but such systems were used solely in the Mediterranean. For a long time two signals were in vogue in the British Royal Navy to call the ship's captains into council and to give the warning 'Enemy in sight'.

Not until the seventeenth century was a code of flag signals employed by the British Navy, but once introduced it developed rapidly, the number of flags and possible signals being increased and the code becoming more complicated.

Toward the end of the eighteenth century a method invented by a French officer was adopted by the British Royal Navy, and a number of improvements were devised. Each flag was assigned a number, and each hoist of one, two, or three flags had a special meaning; a hoist of flags 2, 9 and 1, for

Flags and pennants of the Revised International Code of Signals.

example, meant 'Engage the enemy as closely as possible'.

This numerary method proved insufficient, however, and it was clear that something more flexible was needed. In 1800, adapting a suggestion made by an officer of the East India Company's fleet, Sir Home Popham devised what he called his *Telegraphic Signals* or *Marine Vocabulary,* in which each of the hoists of flags meant not a sentence but a word or even a letter. It included ten flags numbered '1' to '9' and '0'; a 'substitute' flag to repeat one already included in a hoist; and a 'telegraph' flag to show that the vocabulary, and not the older numerary system, was being used.

It was in a development of this code that Nelson gave his famous signal at Trafalgar, his hoists being: the telegraph flag; 253; 269; 863; 261; 471; 958; 220, literally 2, substitute, 0; 370; and 4, 21, 19, 24—the word 'duty', not being included in the vocabulary, had to be spelled out.

In 1804 Sir Home Popham, at the request of the East India Company, adapted his system to meet their needs by compiling a system of *Commercial and Military Signals.* As the Napoleonic Wars were still being waged, it dealt chiefly with

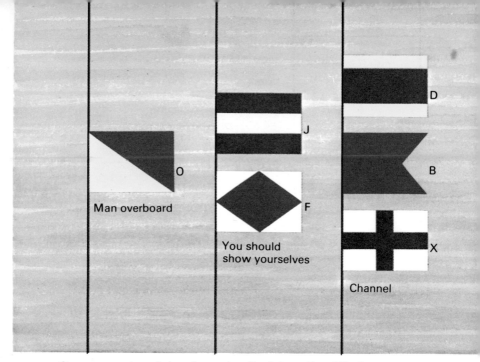

O

Man overboard

J

F

You should
show yourselves

D

B

X

Channel

Some examples of signaling using the International Code.

the requirements of ships sailing in convoy.

After peace had been restored, Captain Frederick Marryat drew up, in 1817, a code for commercial use combining some of the features of the numerary and vocabulary methods. Successful in itself, it also formed a basis for the later, more complicated, signaling codes.

In 1855 a committee appointed by the British Board of Trade reported that such codes were insufficient: ten flags, even with three 'repeaters', using not more than four flags in one hoist, could provide only 9999 different signals. Instead of ten numerary flags, the *Commercial Code of Signals for the Use of All Nations,* which the committee published in 1857, used eighteen flags, each known not by a number but by a letter. Only the consonants were used, however, for to include the vowels could involve the risk that the four flags of a hoist might spell out some obscenity.

Though this code made nearly 80,000 different hoists possible, it was found to be inadequate, and in 1899 another Board of Trade committee produced the First International

2nd substitute (J)
London

Glasgow

Swansea

Code of Signals. This provided a flag for every letter of the alphabet, any hoists which might spell obscenities being avoided; thus over 375,000 different signals could be made.

Even this code proved unsatisfactory, however, and in 1927 an International Radio Telegraph Conference decided to leave its revision to Great Britain, assisted by representatives of several other governments. The revised International code includes not only the twenty-six flags and the 'code and answering pennant' but ten numeral flags and three substitutes, triangular flags for repeating letters or figures.

The British Naval Code, which harmonizes with that of the other member-states of the North Atlantic Treaty Organization, is even more complicated. To the twenty-six alphabetical flags, the ten numeral flags, the three substitutes, and the code and answering pennants, a fourth substitute, nine special flags and eleven special pennants are added, thus enabling an incredible variety of signals to be made.

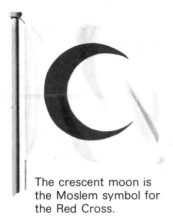

The crescent moon is the Moslem symbol for the Red Cross.

Only Iran uses this emblem for the Red Cross organization.

INTERNATIONAL FLAGS

Unlike those of ancient Greece, the modern Olympic Games are international. It was not until they were resumed after World War II that their flag was hoisted. It displays, on a white field, the symbol of unity, a chain. The colors of its links were probably chosen because they are those most frequently used on the world's flags rather than to represent the world's five continents or races (see page 98).

In 1859 Jean Henri Dunant, a Swiss, was so horrified at the wounds inflicted at the Battle of Solferino that he urged the formation of organized bodies to aid the wounded in wartime. Through his work the first Geneva Convention in 1864 agreed that the wounded and the medical services should be given neutrality. Durant had also argued that the medical services should have their own flag, and the conference adopted the Swiss flag with colors reversed as the Red Cross emblem.

In Moslem countries, where the cross is identified as a Christian symbol, the red crescent takes its place, although in Iran the device is the lion and sun, also in red. Different as they are, these flags are one in their aim: to symbolize the relief of suffering everywhere, in war and in peace.

Consisting of representatives from almost every state, the United Nations Organization was formed in 1945. Its flag bears a map of the world, white on blue; in the center are the continents, seas and North Pole on the Greenwich meridian; on each side appears the symbol of peace, the olive branch.

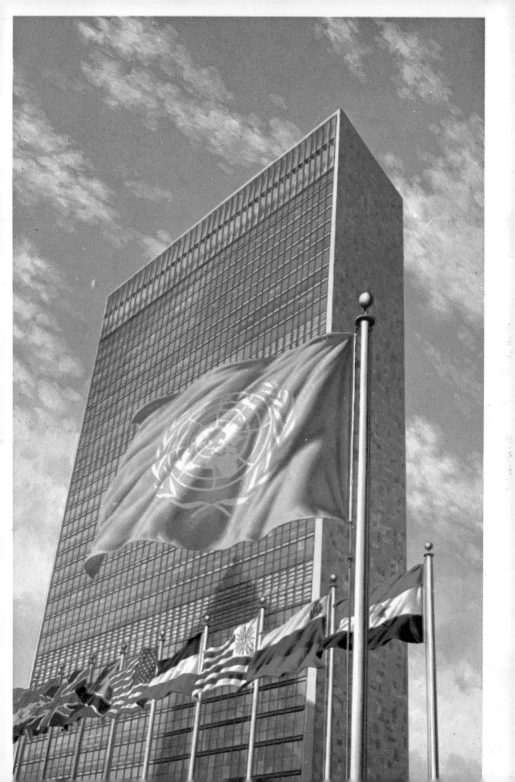

BOOKS TO READ

Flags of the World revised by Capt. E. M. C. Barraclough. London: Frederick Warne, 1965.

The Books of Flags by Admiral G. Campbell and I. O. Evans. Fifth edition, Oxford University Press, 1965.

Flags of All Nations. Mary Elting and Franklin Folsom. Grosset & Dunlap, 1967.

Flags of the World. H. G. Carr. Warne and Company, 1961.

History of the United States Flag. M. M. Quaife. Harper & Row, New York, 1961.

Flags of the U.S.A. Eggenberger. Crowell, 1959.

Boutell's Heraldry revised by C. W. Scott-Giles and J. P. Brooke-Little. London: Frederick Warne, 1966.

British Flags. W. G. Perrin. London: Cambridge Naval and Military Series, Cambridge University Press, 1922.

Colours and Standards in the Royal Air Force. Her Majesty's Stationery Office, 1957.

Flags for Ship Modellers and Marine Artists. A. A. Purves. London: Percival Marshall, 1950.

Flag of Stars. F. Cayley. Melbourne: Rigby, 1966.

Flags over South Africa. R. Gerard. Pretoria Technical College, Pretoria, 1952.

Observer's Book of Flags. I. O. Evans. Observer Pocket Series. London: Frederick Warne, 1959.

Sea-Flags: Their General Use. Comdr. H. P. Mead. Glasgow: Brown, Son & Ferguson, 1938.

Standards, Guidons and Colours of the Commonwealth Force. Major T. J. Edwards. Aldershot: Gale & Polden, 1953.

Yacht Flags and Ensigns. Captain E. M. C. Barraclough. London: Iliffe Books, 1951.

INDEX

THE PROPERTY OF
PALMERSTON AVE. PUBLIC
SCHOOL
Book No. ....

OTHER TITLES IN THE SERIES

The GROSSET ALL-COLOR GUIDES provide a library of authoritative information for readers of all ages. Each comprehensive text with its specially designed illustrations yields a unique insight into a particular area of man's interests and culture.

NOW AVAILABLE

SOON TO BE PUBLISHED